5,000 SIMPLE WORD PROMPTS

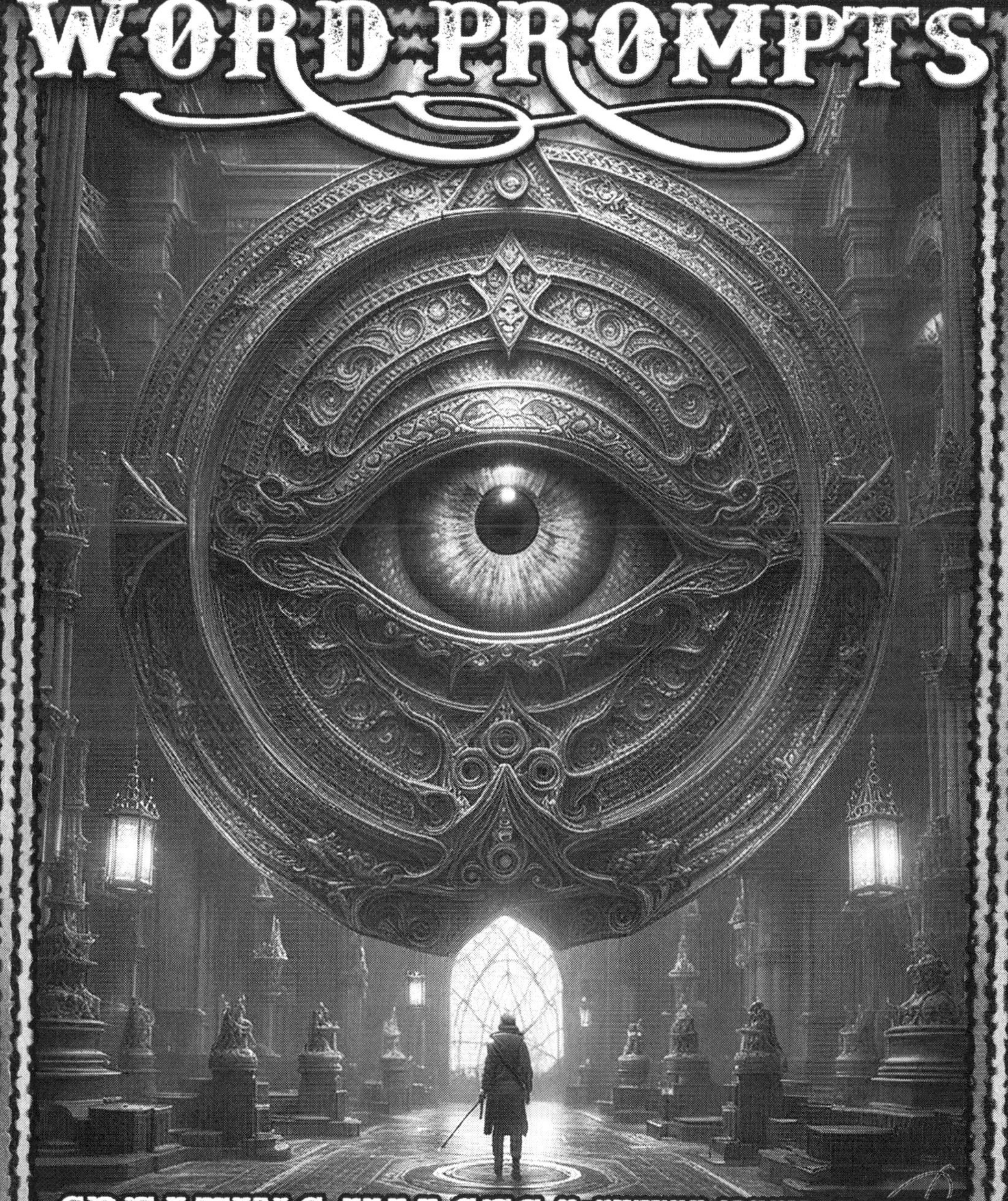

CREATING IMAGES WITH PHRASES

RICHARD MARVIN VOIGT - RIVO

TITLE: 5000 SIMPLE WORD PROMPTS
Sub Title: Creating Images With Phrases

Page Count: 106 pages – 28,095 Words
ISBN-13: 978-1-940961-60-6
ISBN-10: 1940961-60-2

Cover Design, Artwork & Prompts were created & compiled by artist using the latest technology provided by OpenAI, ChatGPT and AI Art Generators actually utilized by Richard Marvin Voigt -RIVO. Lynn Voigt provided proofing and editing services via RIVO Books,

First Printing 2024 LTY-MTT4EvR5-12
Printed in the United States of America

DEDICATION

This publication is dedicated to my incredible loving wife and my ultimate friend, Lynn, who has always supported my entire career interests. She has truly been my guardian angel here on Earth for nearly 60 years, as of this publication, teaching me the true meaning of unconditional love and love of family. She has always been, and always will be, the inspiration, passion and light of my life.

With love to our three gifted and talented children, Lace, Keye & Skye, through difficult times of balancing work and spending quality time together, even with an endless parade of friends with whom they eagerly brought home. Now, we continue to watch each of them grow, prosper, and find their way through life, getting to love them even more deeply, enjoying them as friends.

I also dedicate this publication to our amazing grandson Logan who finds time to spend with his GMa & GPa, who somehow turned 19 overnight. I also wish to thank Lace's hard-working husband Scott for his kind patience, along with Angie's hugs and Lindsay's smiles, plus my lovely baby sister Barbara and her husband Dave. Last but not least, I dedicate this publication to the thousands of creative students who allowed me to be their teacher, not only in art class, but throughout life (far too many to properly list here).

I will leave this earthly body a blessed man who will never be able to fully express my deepest love and gratitude to you all. May each of our spirits live on through endless kind thoughts and lots of great memories, as it should be for all humanity. Thank You All!

I'd Like To Present You With My Quotes From My Human Perspective:

"Creative Thought Is The Only Reality,
Everything Else Is Merely The By-Product Of That Thought"

"Words Come Out Of My Mouth, Before I Can Say Them"

"I Don't Subscribe To Earth Age Nor It's Magazine Subscription."

The Quality Of The Question Asked,
Predetermines The Quality Of The Answer Received"

"If It Isn't FUN – It Isn't Worth Doing – AMEN!"

"Art Is More Than Just A Noun, It's A Verb To Be Seen, Then Understood"

"Keep The Love Growing Creatively"

May You Be Blessed With Great Health, Prosperity & Love!
Richard Marvin Voigt - RIVO

About The Author

Richard Marvin Voigt, aka RIVO, has been fascinated with computers and digital art since the mid-1980s working with early Atari and Commodore personal computers. His friends call him Ricky V. Now, at the age of 82, he's had an award-winning career as a classroom educator and art specialist with Milwaukee Public Schools for nearly 30-years. He's earned recognition and awards for his innovative artwork and has co-published over 90 books and journals while team-teaching with his beautiful wife Lynn at the University of Wisconsin's Osher and Waukesha County Technical College LIR programs, local libraries, churches, businesses & non-profit organizations.

He's had the pleasure of working with thousands of students, many colleagues, artists, models, and local businesses while pursuing his personal passion for creating visual works of fine art as a very prolific artist who shares many interests. He created a unique doodling technique that shows even those who claim they can't draw, drawing in a matter of minutes. One of his projects is called the 'Digital Quilt Series" which currently consists of over 1,700 digital compositions. Each composition is designed to be 38" x 38" that when place end-to-end, span the length of over 17, yes, seventeen football fields, and can be arranged in endless two and three-dimensional configurations.

Over the past couple of years, Richard has ventured into the exciting and intriguing world of AI Art generation exploring existing potential. This massive publication is but a brief example of his research and experimentation as he produces and prints an amazing collection of digital fine art. When asked, he refers to his art as a VERB, not merely a Noun.. While he no longer publicly exhibits his works, he continues to create and print nearly every day as a gift to his wife. Over the past 25+ years, his massive private art collection has grown substantially. Since he doesn't create for monetary gain, he chooses not to sell or market his work other than show earlier works on his websites. It is his final wish that only after his passing, will his entire collection be shown and eventually donated to a worthy organization to remain part of their permanent collection.

Richard and Lynn Voigt are also inventors who hold patent (No. 6,322,878) presented to the Mattel Toy Corporation, and other related toy companies via their agent in California. They're also UW-extension SEW Master Gardeners, teaching classes and giving private tours of their eclectic experimental gardens surrounding their home, producing nearly 1,100 videos for their Wisconsin Garden YouTube channel seen by over 6 million viewers, gaining a faithful following with tens of thousands of subscribers from over 130 countries worldwide.

As history continues to record the imaginative works of artists and the art movements they helped create, we must recognize the influence of technology and its impact upon the arts. Whether a rock, chisel, wood, paint, canvas or a holographic paint brush, every technological advancement played a direct role in what is now possible. While many artist's early works were dismissed by formality and ignorance as to what art is or should be, many of those early rejected works are now revered and eagerly sold for millions. Gifted artist creates from within completing a vision. Like Ricky V, we continually enter exciting creative portals to unlimited visions. Today is always the first day of your new reality, so claim yours TODAY!

WHAT IS ARTIFICAL INTELLIGENCE TECHNOLOGY ANYWAY?

If you're new to areas of Artificial Intelligence, there are some additional things you should know continuing your education within this industry which are already part of your daily life. In today's world we all need to continue educating ourselves, especially in the area of technological advancements. Here is a brief introduction to three areas of amazing technology that continues to grow and expand, as should each of us. Here's some terms you need to know, if you don't already.

OpenAI, ChatGPT, and AI Art Generations represent the latest cutting-edge advancements in the field of artificial intelligence (AI) technology, with applications ranging from natural language understanding and communication to creative content generation and artistic expression.

It helps when one understands the basic concepts of Open AI, ChatGPT and AI Art Generators in encouraging you to gain a greater understanding of this amazing technology as programming it expands. I'll discuss my experiences with these areas of Artificial Intelligence (AI) including what I've learned, created and published. You'll have the opportunity to see unique examples of digital art, video productions and personal publications at **www.ART262.com.**

OpenAI is a research organization dedicated to developing artificial intelligence (AI) technology in a safe and beneficial manner. It aims to advance the field of AI and make its benefits widely accessible to humanity. OpenAI conducts research in various areas of AI, including natural language processing, reinforcement learning, computer vision, and robotics. The organization also releases open-source software and publishes research papers to contribute to the advancement of AI technology globally.

ChatGPT is a conversational AI model developed by OpenAI it's now expanded to version 3.5. It uses deep learning techniques to understand and generate human-like text responses based on input provided by users. ChatGPT can engage in conversations on a wide range of topics, answer questions, provide explanations, and even offer suggestions. It powers chatbots, virtual assistants, and other applications where human-like interaction is desired, such as customer support, language translation, and educational platforms. VISIT: https://chat.openai.com/chat

AI Art Generations refer to the use of AI algorithms and neural networks to create, modify, or enhance visual artworks. These algorithms can generate new images, transform existing images into different styles, or assist artists in the creative process. AI Art Generators leverage techniques such as deep learning, generative adversarial networks (GANs), and style transfer to produce visually compelling and diverse artwork. They can be used for various purposes, including digital art creation, photo editing, image synthesis, and visual effects generation. AI Art Generators have sparked interest and experimentation among artists, designers, photographers, and enthusiasts, offering new possibilities for creative expression and exploration. We'll show you some to explore.

To Infinity & Beyond - Is Real!

Here Are Several Unique Considerations Marking A Distinctive Shift In The Way Art Is Created Which Can Make The Results From AI Art Generation Truly Amazing.

Algorithmic Creativity:
Generative Algorithms: AI art generation relies on generative algorithms that can produce new and unique pieces of art based on patterns and information learned from existing data.

Non-deterministic Output: The algorithms introduce an element of randomness, allowing for a wide range of creative outputs, making each piece of generated art unique.

Learning from Data:
Machine Learning Techniques: AI art generation often employs machine learning models, such as neural networks, which learn patterns and styles from vast datasets of existing artworks.

Adaptive Improvement: These models continuously improve their ability to generate art by learning from a diverse range of artistic styles, genres, and techniques.

Collaboration with Artists:
Human-AI Collaboration: Many AI art projects involve collaboration between artists and AI algorithms. The AI serves as a tool or a source of inspiration for artists to enhance their creative process. Amplifying

Artistic Vision: AI can amplify an artist's vision by suggesting new ideas, styles, or even completing parts of an artwork based on the artist's input.

Exploration of Unconventional Styles:
Cross-Stylistic Creativity: AI can seamlessly blend and experiment with various artistic styles, pushing the boundaries of what is traditionally possible in art creation.

Emergence of New Styles: AI art generation can lead to the emergence of entirely new and unconventional artistic styles that may not have been explored before.

Accessibility and Democratization:
Artistic Tools for All: AI art generation tools are becoming increasingly accessible, allowing individuals without traditional art training to engage in the creative process.

Democratizing Creativity: AI-driven art democratizes creativity, enabling a broader range of people to express themselves artistically and participate in the creation of unique artworks.

AI's Interpretation of Creativity:
Machine Understanding of Aesthetics: AI algorithms can be trained to understand and interpret aesthetic principles, leading to the creation of art that aligns with human perceptions of beauty.

Beyond Imitation: AI doesn't merely imitate existing styles; it can reinterpret and synthesize elements to produce novel and innovative artworks.

Dynamic and Evolving Art:
Real-Time Adaptation: AI art generation can adapt in real-time to user input, creating a dynamic and interactive artistic experience.

Continuous Evolution: AI algorithms can be updated and improved over time, ensuring a continuous evolution of artistic capabilities and styles.

Ethical Considerations:
Ownership and Authorship: The question of ownership and authorship arises as AI contributes significantly to the creation process. Discussions around the attribution of creative work in collaborations between AI and humans are ongoing.

WHY AI IMAGE GENERATORS CONTINUE GETTING SMARTER & SMARTER

The future of Artificial Intelligence (AI) image generators holds promising possibilities for creating amazing imagery even from simple word and phrase prompts. Even single words now show great promise. When I started creating AI images several years ago, I had to refine the vision I had roaming around inside my head and figure out all the keywords I could think of. Some prompts became a paragraph - YIKES! My first book, *13,000 AI Prompts Turning Words Into Visions,* shares much longer prompt sentences. My second book, *5555 FUN & FUNNY PROMPTS Turning Words Into Images*, began shortening my fun and silly prompts which led me to create my third book: *5000 SIMPLE WORD PROMPTS - Creating Images With Phrases*, simplifying prompts to short phrases with results that are equally impressive. As AI technologies continue to advance, we can expect to see more refined developments in each of these areas:

Improved Image Quality: AI image generators will continue becoming more adept at producing high-quality and realistic images based on simple prompts. With advancements in machine learning algorithms and access to vast datasets, these generators can refine their understanding of visual concepts and produce more visually appealing results.

Enhanced Creativity: AI models are increasingly capable of understanding and interpreting creative prompts, allowing them to generate imaginative and unique imagery. As AI systems become more sophisticated, they may develop the ability to incorporate artistic principles and styles into their generated images, leading to even more stunning and creative results.

Personalization and Customization: AI image generators could offer personalized and customized imagery tailored to individual preferences and needs. Users may be able to provide specific criteria or preferences, such as color schemes, styles, or themes, and the AI generator could generate images accordingly, providing a more personalized experience.

Integration with Other Technologies: AI image generators may integrate with other emerging technologies, such as augmented reality (AR) and virtual reality (VR), to create immersive and interactive visual experiences. This integration could enable users to interact with and manipulate generated imagery in real-time, opening up new possibilities for creative expression and storytelling.

Ethical and Social Considerations: As AI image generators become more powerful, ethical and social considerations surrounding their use will become increasingly important. It will be crucial to address issues related to copyright, authenticity, bias, and the potential misuse of AI-generated imagery to ensure that these technologies are used responsibly and ethically.

Remember, AI Image Generators can inspire artists by generating amazing images, novel ideas, visual concepts, and stylistic variations that artists may not have considered. They serve as creative tools for exploration and experimentation, sparking new directions and possibilities in artistic expression.

The future of AI image generators holds immense potential for transforming creative expression and visual storytelling. With ongoing advancements in AI technology and continued research and development efforts, we can expect to see even more impressive and innovative applications of AI-generated imagery in the years to come.

Despite the controversy over machine learning, art generation represents a convergence of smarter technology expanding artistic expression with unlimited possibilities and challenges in the ever-evolving landscape of creative endeavors. Its uniqueness lies in the blend of computational power, learning algorithms, and human creativity, pushing the boundaries of what 'Art' can be. Now you can make the final decision for yourself.

Image generators can augment artists' creative capabilities by providing alternative perspectives, stylistic influences, and compositional suggestions. Artists can leverage AI-generated content as a source of inspiration and a catalyst for creative innovation.

AI generators can help streamline certain aspects of the artistic process, such as sketching, rendering, and composition, thereby saving artists time and effort. They can automate repetitive tasks, generate preliminary designs, and assist artists in refining their ideas more efficiently.

It's also providing accessibility and inclusivity to artistic tools and resources, making creative expression more accessible and inclusive to individuals with diverse backgrounds, skill levels, and abilities. They empower aspiring artists to explore their artistic potential and participate in the creative community.

Within the workforce, they enable collaborative and co-creative interactions between artists and AI systems, fostering interdisciplinary collaborations, and expanding the boundaries of artistic collaboration. Artists can collaborate with AI systems to co-create artworks, explore new artistic techniques, and push the boundaries of artistic innovation.

AI art generators represent a transformative paradigm shift in the creative process, offering artists new opportunities for exploration, inspiration, efficiency, and collaboration. As AI technologies continue to evolve and mature, the value of AI art generators to artists is expected to grow, shaping the future of artistic expression and creative innovation in diverse and exciting ways.

As mentioned, over the past couple of years I've been experimenting with a wide variety of word prompts. I began with prompts loaded with keywords that defined my vision and soon realized that using simple word prompts began creating unexpected and surprising results. While I'm not advocating eliminating complex loaded keyword prompts, I understand that as AI expands it's learning capabilities, sometimes less produces more than anticipated.

For the purposes of this book, I decided to share some very simple word phrases collected from a variety of animals, clichés, creatures, flowers, foods, games, movies, mythology, philosophy, places, poems, songs, along with a variety of additional universal and futuristic ideas.

Remember, the purpose of this list of simple word phrase prompts is to get your juices flowing and expand image generation possibilities. This list is merely a starting point in exploring prompt engineering and the images they create. Always feel free to add your ideas, your choice keywords, and add them to augment and expand them in a way that best serves your prompting requirements.

SO HOW DO ARTIFICIAL INTELLIGENCE (AI) ART GENERATORS WORK?

Imagine a magical machine that can make beautiful pictures or drawings all by itself using Prompts. An image generator is basically a computer program that uses artificial intelligence algorithms to create original works of art, such as paintings, drawings, or digital images. These algorithms analyze patterns, styles, and compositions from existing databases, then generates new original images. AI has now added another amazing tool in every artist's tool belt, harnessing the power of machine learning and computational creativity, to produce original artistic content autonomously.

Using your creative imagination and lots of powerful keyword Prompts, you can now create something truly incredible. It's like giving your magical machine a stronger creative idea each time, then watching it turn your ideas into colorful and beautiful images, drawings or designs, just like magic.

While most of us may have little or no coding skills, it's still a lot of fun learning and creating AI Art. For those still curious, here's a partial sampling of an AI Art generated algorithm code:

```
import tensorflow as tf
import numpy as np
import PIL.Image

# Load the pre-trained Inception model
base_model =
tf.keras.applications.InceptionV3(include_top=False,
weights='imagenet')

# Choose a layer to maximize activations
names = ['mixed3', 'mixed5']
layers = [base_model.get_layer(name).output for name
in names]

# Create the feature extraction model
dream_model =
tf.keras.Model(inputs=base_model.input,
outputs=layers)

def calc_loss(img, model):
# Pass the image through the model to get feature
activations
img_batch = tf.expand_dims(img, axis=0)
layer_activations = model(img_batch)

losses = []
for act in layer_activations:
loss = tf.math.reduce_mean(act)
losses.append(loss)

return tf.reduce_sum(losses)

def deepdream(model, img, steps=100, step_size=0.01):
for step in range(steps):
with tf.GradientTape() as tape:
# Set the image variable
tape.watch(img)
loss = calc_loss(img, model)

# Calculate the gradient of the loss with respect to the
image
gradients = tape.gradient(loss, img)

# Normalize the gradients
gradients /= tf.math.reduce_std(gradients) + 1e-8

# Update the image with the scaled gradients
img = img + gradients * step_size
img = tf.clip_by_value(img, -1, 1)

return img.numpy()

def run_deep_dream_simple(img, steps=100,
step_size=0.01):
img = tf.keras.preprocessing.image.img_to_array(img)
img =
tf.keras.applications.inception_v3.preprocess_input(img
)

img = tf.constant(img)
img = deepdream(dream_model, img, steps=steps,
step_size=step_size)

img = tf.keras.preprocessing.image.array_to_img(img)
return img

#
Example usage
image_path = 'path/to/your/image.jpg'
original_img = PIL.Image.open(image_path)
dream_img =
run_deep_dream_simple(img=original_img, steps=100,
step_size=0.01)

# Display the original and generated images
original_img.show()
dream_img.show()
```

HERE ARE SEVERAL INTERESTING AI ART GENERATOR WEBSITES:

https://nightcafe.studio/	https://palette.fm/
https://openai.com/product/dall-e-2/	https://picsart.com/ai-image-generator/
https://www.bing.com/create/	https://replicate.com/pixray/text2image/
https://dreamstudio.ai/	https://runwayml.com/
https://www.midjourney.com/	https://rytr.me/
https://openart.ai/create/	https://stablecog.com/
https://app.prodia.com/	https://starryai.com/
https://deepai.org/	https://vanceai.com/image-generator/
https://deepdreamgenerator.com/	https://writesonic.com/
https://dream.ai/	https://www.artbreeder.com/
https://firefly.adobe.com/	https://www.canva.com/ai-image-generator/
https://getimg.ai/	https://www.craiyon.com/
https://land.prisma-ai.com/magic-avatars/	https://www.creativefabrica.com/spark/
https://letsenhance.io/	https://www.fotor.com/images/create/
	https://www.jasper.ai/art/
	https://www.tryleap.ai/

https://apps.apple.com/us/app/artout-ai-image-generator/
https://www.gettyimages.com/ai/generation/create/
https://www.myheritage.com/ai-time-machine/
https://www.shutterstock.com/ai-image-generator/

You will find many apps and websites that help beginners and advanced users create amazing ideas faster than it took me to write this sentence. But no matter which app or website you choose to use, it will be your unique use of power word prompts that will determine the image quality you create.

NightCafe isn't the only AI Art Generator you should consider testing, but it's one I have been using for several years that produces great image results. You may want to visit their website before deciding to proceed.

For demonstration purposes I'll use NightCafe for Generating AI Images

CREATE A NEW ACCOUNT AT: https://creator.nightcafe.studio/
SIGN UP IS FREE Simply Provide A User Name, Email Address & Strong Password
ALWAYS KEEP YOUR PASSWORDS SAFE & PRIVATE

At the time of this writing, New Accounts receive 50 FREE Credits in their Account
PLUS 5 FREE Credits each day – So, check your email daily
Then you can start creating a new image for generally 1 credit.

HERE'S SOME HELPFUL NIGHTCAFE STEP-BY-STEP INSTRUCTIONS:

PREPARATION – OPEN ALL FILES AS NEEDED:
Open Your NightCafe Account - resize your viewing monitor windows as needed:
Open My Computer – Select an internal or external hard drive and open said drive
Create a new AI IMAGE Folder & give it a Name you'll remember
Keep Folder Open for upcoming images and text downloads
Create and Title a new WORD doc for keeping track of all your new word PROMPTS
Find and Open your DOWNLOAD FOLDER found under your C Drive desktop listing
(Optional) Open NOTEBOOK where you can write, copy and paste items

YOU CAN USE ANY SIMPLE PROMPTS TO CREATE AMAZING IMAGES
It could be as simple as using just a Subject: "WHITE DAISIES" and nothing more.

Or you could expand your simple phrase prompt by adding
(Verbs & Descriptive Adjectives & Adverbs) and additional KEYWORDS

Adding These To Your Basic PROMPT Could Look Something Like This:
"WHITE DAISIES in a Blue Vase, in the style of Van Gogh

THEN ADD MY 'SECRET SAUCE' KEYWORDS AFTER EACH SIMPLE PROMPT
, Epic, 3D, Hyper-Realistic, Hyper-Detailed, Hyper-Colorful, Atmospheric, Cinematic Lighting"

THE FINAL PROMPT READY TO CREATE MIGHT THEN LOOK LIKE THIS
"White Daisies in a Blue Vase, in the style of Van Gogh, Epic, 3D, Hyper-Realistic, Hyper-Detailed, Hyper Colorful, Atmospheric, Cinematic Lighting"

White Daisies

Sun Flowers

Bearded Iris

These were created by my wife, Lynn at her very first attempt using an AI Image Generator.
The originals were in color, but I turned them Black & White for this publication.

SO, IF YOU'RE READY, HERE'S SOME HELPFUL STEP-BY-STEP INSTRUCTIONS:
(REMEMBER TO SAVE AFTER EVERY CHANGE)

HERE'S HOW YOU START GENERATING IMAGES?

1. **Open NightCafe – Click the red CREATE button (TOP BAR Upper Right)**

2. **Write out your NEW PROMPT IDEA – SAVE in your WORD DOC**

3. **Locate add TEXT PROMPT (Left Create Column) on NightCafe Page**

4. **Copy & Paste OR Write your own PROMPT Into TEXT PROMPT box that says 'Type Something'**

5. **Select MODEL (little side >) SDXL 1.0, Juggernaut XL, etc. Test different ones**

6. **Select STYLE (side arrow >) NightCafe, Hyperreal, Epic, Dark Fantasy, Artistic Portrait, etc.**

7. **Select Number of Images (Always select '1' when testing a new prompt)**

8. **Select SETTINGS (side arrow >) and your desired size format 1:1 Square Images, or 3:4 Vertical Rectangle or 4:3 Horizontal Rectangle etc.**

9. **WHEN ALL SETTINGS READY - Click the bottom red "CREATE" button To Start Generating Image**

10. **When Image Appears and you want to SAVE IT move your mouse over the bottom of image and look for the downward image arrow under image**

11. **Click & Select DOWNLOAD IMAGE – It begins automatically saving your Selected Image to your computer's download folder**

12. **Open your 'This PC' and locate your computer's Download Folder Highly Recommend RETITLING Image(s) Now**

13. **Transfer this image from Download Folder To Your AI IMAGE FOLDER HOLD DOWN LEFT MOUSE KEY & DRAG Image into your FOLDER**

14. **You will need photo editing software (Photoshop etc.) to edit your images**

ALWAYS KEEP IN MIND – EACH WORD ADDED TO A PROMPT HAS POWER
You may need to constantly tweak your prompts by adding more descriptive power words while eliminating fluff words that have little meaning or value to the completion of the composition you have in mind. Word prompts help one expand their vocabulary very quickly. I've prepared a list of power words to add to your prompts a little later in this publication, words charged with commanding emotion.

PROMPT SIZING: For Example - Night Cafe offers "More Settings" option
Number of images: 1, 4, 9, & 16 at a time
Output Resolution changes based on Generator Model selected
Runtime: Short costs 1 credit, medium costs 1.25 credits, or long costs 1.5 credits
1:1 Square (**DEFAULT SETTING)** ***Change This Setting Any Of These Sizes That You Want:***
3:4 Vertical Rectangle
4:3 Horizontal Rectangle
9:16 Tall Vertical, and **16:9** Wide Horizontal, etc.

I remember a woman criticizing entries in my first book that used **ar 4:3**, etc, in several prompts. She thought I was promoting a secret code that meant automatic rifle into my prompts. This is why taking time to understand how AI really works becomes very useful.

OTHER SYSTEMS FOR PROMPT SIZING
Image Aspect Ratio Sizing: **(ar) represents proportions - not automatic rifle**
Depending of the Image Generation you use, these may also show up as options:

ar-9:16	Often used for mobile or vertical size ratios
ar-10:16	This may be great for a portrait
ar-4:3	Commonly used as aspect ratio for 35mm celluloid film, TVs and monitors
ar-4:5	Perhaps more appropriate for creating an Instagram type portrait
ar-2:1	The Univisium ratio is a compromise between cinema screens and TV screens,
now	famous in video streaming.

OTHER CHOICES IN ADJUSTING YOUR WORD PROMPTS
Type in a full descriptive Prompt Word(s) sentence, as if you were writing a caption for a photo. Include as much detail as you see fit, including colors, styles, and emotions. Then click the CREATE button to generate your image

Some AI Generators allow you to use multiple prompts that varying weights.
Use weights to include or exclude specific concepts from your image.
Weight values should typically be in the range from -2.0 to +2.0.
Weights are optional, but most have a default of 1.0.

© 2024

Generated Art by
RIVO

It's important to acknowledge AI when exhibiting or printing generated images.
This is a symbol sticker I created and add to all of my AI prints

CONSIDER ADDING This To Your Prompts - *IN THE STYLE OF* AN ARTISTS' NAME:

Examples *"Oil Painting in the style if* or *Abstract Rendering in the style of" or:*

Realistic Rendering in the style of:* or simply: *In The Style of:

OR BY ADDING *IN THE STYLE OF* YOUR FAVORITE ARTIST

Alberto Vargas
Alphonse Mucha
Andy Warhol
Anish Kapoor
Bob Ross
Cai Guo-Qiang
Camille Pissaro
Caravaggio
Chuck Close
Claude Monet
Damien Ortega
David Hockney
Diego Velázquez
Edvard Munch
Edward Hopper
Eugene Delacroix
Frida Kahlo

Georgia O'Keeffe
Goerge Seurat
Grandma Moses
Gustav Klimt
Henri Matisse
JM William Turner
Jackson Pollock
James Audubon
Jan Van Eyck
Jean Baptiste Monge
Jeff Koons
Johannes Vermeer
John Constable
Joseph Mallord
Kwame Brathwaite
Leonardo Da Vinci
Liu Xiaodong

Mariko Mori
Mary Cassatt
Michelangelo
Pablo Picasso
Paul Cezanne
Paul Rubens
Augsste Renoir
Pieter Bruegel-Elder
Rembrandt
Rene Magritte
Roy Lichtenstein
Salvador Dali
Sandro Botticelli
Thomas Cole
Tim Burton
Victor Hugo
Vincent Van Gogh
Walt Disney
William Turner
Yoko Ono

OR BY ADDING - *IN THE STYLE OF* AN ILLUSTRATORS' NAME:

Sir John Tenniel 1820-1914 English	Aubrey Beardsley 1872-1898 English
Walter Crane 1845-1915 English	J.C. Leyendecker 1874-1951 American
Kate Greenaway 1846-1901 English	Violet Oakley 1874-1961 American Muralist
Edwin Austin Abbey 1852-1911 American	Ivan Bilibin 1876-1942 Russian
Howard Pyle 1853-1911 American	Harrison Fisher 1877-1934 American
Louis John Rhead 1858-1926 English	James Montgomery Flagg 1877-1960 American
Jessie Willcox Smith 1863-1935 American	Frank E. Schoonover 1877-1972 American
Edward Penfield 1866-1925 American	Millicent Sowerby 1878-1967 English
Beatrix Potter 1866-1943 English	C. Coles Phillips 1880-1927 American
Charles Dana Gibson 1867-1944 American	Joseph Clement Coll 1881-1921 American
Arthur Rackham 1867-1939 English	Edmund Dulac 1882-1953 French
Maxfield Parrish 1870-1966 American	N.C. Wyeth 1882-1945 American
Charles Robinson 1870-1937	Edward Julius Detmold 1883-1957 English
Elizabeth Shippen Green 1871-1954 American	Kay Nielsen 1886-1957 Danish/American
	OR YOUR FAVORITES

OR BY ADDING - *IN THE STYLE OF* A FASHION DESIGNERS' NAME:

Alexander McQueen	Enzoani	Naeem Khan
Alice + Olivia	Galia Lahav	Nicole Miller
Amsale	Giambattista Valli	Oscar de la Renta
Anne Barge	Givenchy	Prada
Badgley Mischka	Gucci	Pronovias
Balmain	Hayley Paige	Rachel Gilbert
BCBG Max Azria	J. Mendel	Ralph & Russo
Berta Bridal	Jenny Packham	Reem Acra
BHLDN	Jenny Yoo	Romona
Carolina Herrera	Justin Alexander	Rosa Clará
Chanel	Lela Rose	Tadashi Shoji
David's Bridal	Maggie Sottero	Temperley London
Dior	Marchesa	Tom Ford
Elie by Elie Saab	Michael Kors	Valentino
Elie Saab	Monique Lhuillier	Vera Wang
		Versace
		Watters
		YolanCris

ALSO EXPLORE ADDING UNIQUE BACKGROUNDS TO YOUR PROMPTS

- Solid White Background
- Solid Black Background
- Solid Color Background
- White Crumpled Paper
- Black Textured Paper
- Gradient Paper Background
- Muslin Background
- Canvas Background
- Textured Fabric Background
- Velvet Background
- Silk Fabric Background
- Burlap Background
- Woodgrain Background
- Brick Wall Background
- Stone Wall Background
- Concrete Wall Background
- Weathered Door Background
- Distressed Wood Background
- Graffiti Wall Background
- Urban Street Background
- Industrial Warehouse Background
- Autumn Leaves Background
- Spring Blossoms Background
- Summer Field Background
- Winter Snow Background
- Tropical Beach Background
- Watercolor Background
- Abstract Painted Background
- Oil Painting Background
- Galaxy Background
- Starry Night Background
- Cloudscape Background

- Mountain Landscape Background
- Desert Dunes Background
- Ocean Waves Background
- Underwater Background
- City Skyline Background
- Sunset Gradient Background
- Sunrise Gradient Background
- Rainbow Background
- Retro Wallpaper Background
- Vintage Textile Background
- Shabby Chic Background
- Lace Background
- Polka Dot Background
- Striped Background
- Chevron Background
- Plaid Background
- Herringbone Background
- Damask Background
- Moroccan Tile Background
- Celtic Knot Background
- Floral Print Background
- Botanical Garden Background
- Macro Flower Background
- Fern Leaves Background
- Tropical Foliage Background
- Mossy Forest Floor Background
- Rustic Wooden Floor Background
- Victorian Wallpaper Background
- Star Wars-inspired Background
- Harry Potter-inspired Background

- Sci-fi Futuristic Background
- Cyberpunk City Background
- Steampunk Gear Background
- Vintage Bookshelf Background
- Antique Map Background
- Glitter Backgrounds
- Bokeh Lights Background
- Colorful Gradient Background
- Water Ripple Background
- Sand Dunes Background
- Rusty Metal Background
- Gothic Architecture Background
- Sports Stadium Background
- Urban Graffiti Background
- Vintage Car Background
- Retro Diner Background
- Movie Theater Background
- Casino Table Background
- Christmas Tree Background
- Hanukkah Celebration Background
- Diwali Festival Background
- Easter Egg Background
- Halloween Spooky Forest Background
- Thanksgiving Feast Background
- Valentine's Day Hearts Background
- 4th of July Fireworks Background
- New Year's Eve Party Background
- Masquerade Ball Background

Circus Tent Background
Pirate Ship Background
Fairy Tale Castle Background
Vintage Plane Background
Police Lineup Background
Jail Cell Background
Ancient Ruins Background
Spaceship Interior Background
Underworld Cavern Background
Japanese Garden Background
Tea Ceremony Background
Samurai Dojo Background
Sushi Bar Background
Balloon Festival Background
Butterfly Garden Background
Candyland Background
Driftwood Beach Background
Enchanted Forest Background
Gingerbread House Background
Hot Air Balloon Background
Ice Cream Parlor Background
Jellyfish Aquarium Background
Koi Pond Background
Lighthouse Background
Mermaid Underwater Background
Neon Cityscape Background
Origami Paper Crane Background
Parisian Cafe Background
Rainbow Bridge Background

Sakura Blossom Background
Space Shuttle Launch Background
St. Patrick's Shamrock Background
Time Travel Portal Background
Venice Canal Background
Vintage Barber Shop Background
Victorian Ballroom Background
Waterfall Oasis Background
Wizard's Library Background
Zen Garden Background
Art Studio Background
Carnival Ferris Wheel Background
Crystal Cave Background
Dystopian Alley Background
Eiffel Tower Background
Fairy Ring Background
Fantasy Castle Background
Flower Shop Background
Futuristic City Background
Gingerbread Village Background
Grand Staircase Background
Greenhouse Background
Hobbit Hole Background
Ice Palace Background
Irish Pub Background
Library of Alexandria Background
Mad Hatter's Tea Party Background
Moroccan Bazaar Background
Observatory Background
Owl Café Background

Pastel Cloudscape Background
Pumpkin Patch Background
Quaint Village Background
Renaissance Fair Background
Riverboat Casino Background
Rock Concert Background
Roman Colosseum Background
Secret Garden Background
Sky Lantern Festival Background
Space Colony Background
Speakeasy Background
Sports Stadium Background
Steampunk Laboratory Background
Stonehenge Background
Summer Campfire Background
Sunflower Field Background
Superhero City Background
Surreal Cloudscape Background
Taj Mahal Background
Time Square Background
Tokyo Street Background
Underwater Volcano Background
Upside-Down World Background
Victorian Parlor Background
Viking Longhouse Background
Vintage Toy Store Background
Volcanic Lava Flow Background

Watercolor Galaxy Background	**Windmill Countryside Background**	**Zen Bamboo Forest Background**
Winding Forest Path Background	**Winter Village Background**	**Zen Rock Garden Background**
	Yacht Club Background	**Zootopia Cityscape Background**
	Yellowstone National Park	

CONSIDER PLAYING WITH OTHER UNUSUAL SIMPLE AI PROMPT PHRASES:

Algorithmic Phantasmagoria	Esoteric Algorithms	Quantum Conundrum
Algorithmic Serendipity	Esoteric Byte Ballet	Quantum Echoes
Algorithmic Sonnets	Esoteric Data Ballet	Quantum Entanglement
Algorithmic Syllogism	Esoteric Dreams	Quantum Labyrinth
Binary Ballet	Esoteric Phantasmagoria	Quantum Murmurs
Binary Mirage	Esoteric Whispers	Quantum Reverie
Binary Murmurs	Ethereal Algorithms	Quantum Whimsy
Binary Odyssey	Fractal Daydreams	Quantum Whispers
Binary Sonnets	Fractal Dreamscape	Robotic Dreamscape
Binary Symphony	Fractal Echoes	Robotic Kaleidoscope
Binary Whispers	Galactic Whispers	Robotic Paradox
Celestial Algorithms	Holographic Algorithms	Robotic Reverie
Celestial Cipher	Holographic Byte Dance	Robotic Serendipity
Celestial Dreamscape	Holographic Dreamscape	Robotic Sonnets
Celestial Murmurs	Holographic Enigma	Robotic Symphony
Celestial Riddles	Holographic Interlude	Synaptic Dreamscape
Celestial Whispers	Holographic Riddles	Synaptic Enigma
Cerebral Symphony	Holographic Syllogism	Synaptic Kaleidoscope
Cosmic Byte Ballet	Holographic Symphony	Synaptic Murmurs
Cosmic Enigma	Nanoscopic Dreams	Synaptic Phantasmagoria
Cosmic Kaleidoscope	Nanoscopic Whimsy	Synaptic Sonnets
Cosmic Sonnets	Neural Labyrinth	Synaptic Whispers
Cryptic Byte Dance	Neural Paradox	Synthetic Dreamscape
Cybernetic Dreamscape	Neural Serendipity	Techno-Ethereal Odyssey
Cybernetic Serendipity	Neural Syllogism	Techno-Ethereal Riddles
Cybernetic Whimsy	Neural Tapestry	Techno-Ethereal Sonnets
Digital Daydreams	Pixelated Paradox	Techno-Ethereal Whispers
Digital Labyrinth	Pixelated Whispers	Virtual Enigma
Digital Phantasmagoria	Quantum Byte Ballet	Virtual Mirage
Digital Sonnets	Quantum Byte Dance	Virtual Riddles
		Virtual Symphony

You May Also Want To Play Around With Natural Or Really Strange Configurations & Combinations

Your Name,
Friends Name,
Pet or Nickname,
Alpha Numeric Combinations,
Nonsense Words,
Nonsense Alpha Numeric Combinations,
Poetry,
Limericks,
Haikus,
Song Titles,
Book Titles,
Historical Events,
Current Events, Time,
Dreams,
Job Title,
Hobbies,
Foods,
Nature,
Your Neighborhood,
Street Names,
Favorite Cities,
Vacation Destinations,
You get the idea!

- - - HERE ARE SOME OF MY 'SECRET SAUCE' PROMPT KEYWORDS - - -
ADD A COUPLE OF THESE AFTER YOUR PROMPT & SEE WHAT HAPPENS!

2/3 Face Angle
3D
64 Megapixels
8K Resolution
A Masterpiece
Abstract Art
Airy
Architectural
Art Deco
Artstation
Asymmetrical
Atmospheric
Attractive
Beautiful
Behanced HD
Blurred
Bokeh
Brilliant
Canon Lens
Cinema 4D
Cinematic Background
Cinematic Lighting
Circuit Background
Circular
Color Depth
Color Portrait
Colorful
Complementary Colors
Complex
Concept Art
Creative
Dark Fantasy
Deep Colors
Detailed
Digital
Dramatic
Dramatic Lighting
Draw
Drawing
Elaborate
Epic

Exotic
Fantastical
Fantasy
Filigree Patterns
Flowing
Friendly
Frontal View
Full Body
Futuristic
Graffiti Art
Ground Level
Happy
Head And Shoulder
High Contrast
High Fashion Pose
Highly Decorative
Hyper-Colorful
Hyper-Detailed
Hyper-Exotic
Hyper-Realistic
Illuminate
Imaginative
Intricate
Intricate Details
Jewelry
Line Drawing
Lush
Magical
Masks
Matte
Matte Painting
Maximalist
Mech Details
Melting
Metallic
Meticulous
Mid Shot
Neon
Oil Gouache
Oil Painting
Paint

Painterly
Paper Curls Patterns
Pen & Ink
Pencil
Pencil Drawing
Perfect
Perfect Composition
Pointillism
Polished Metal
Polished Metal
Polychromatic
Profile View
Render In Blender
Sad
Scary
Sci-Fi
Screen Art
Sharp Focus
Shot On DSLR
Side Light
Sketch
Smiling
Sparkling
Splash Art
Spray Paint
Street Art
Studio Lighting
Stunning
Stylized
Surreal
Surrealistic
Symmetrical
Torn Paper
Trending In Artsation
Triadic Colors
Tropical
Ultra Details
Ultra Quality
Ultra Realistic
Unreal Engine
Unreal Engine 5
Vibrant
Vibrant Colors
Volume

A WORD OF CAUTION:

Many Filtered Words May Be Banned And Face Prompt Rejection, Words Such As:

Bloody, Injury, Death, Guts, Gory, Gruesome, Torture, Suicide, Cannibalism, Taboo Words, Ethnic Slurs, Phobia Terminology, Slang Nicknames, Sexually Explicit, Nudity, Unclothed, Risqué, Sexual, Genitalia, Private Body Parts, Foreign Sex Words, Sex Slang, XXX, Kill, Exploitation of Children, Inflammatory, Derogatory, Blasphemy, Profanity, Prohibited, Drugs, Alcohol, Cigarettes, Terrorist, or Similar Words In Other Languages **etc… (others may also become blocked)**

Be mindful that each generator has it's own list of banned words. Avoid being banned from their image generating account platform by misuse of their terms of agreement.

Too many attempts in using banned or filtered words could result in being banned from using your selected AI generator. Carefully read the terms of your AI generators' agreement.

FEEL FREE TO CHECK OUT MY AI VIDEO COLLECTION AT:

www.ART262.com

READY TO ENJOY YOUR PROMPTING ADVENTURES? WHEN YOU ARE, STRAP YOURSELF IN FOR UNEXPECTED NEW IMAGE ADVENTURES EVEN WITH USING SIMPLE WORD PHRASE PROMPTS.

Therefore, My Wish For You Is To Enjoy Playing With My "5000 SIMPLE WORD PROMPTS" And Encouraging You To Imagine The Endless Variations You Can Insert, Modify Or Create Yourself.

HERE'S YOUR EXCLUSIVE GUIDE TO RICHARD'S VAULT OF 5000 SIMPLE PHRASE PROMPTS

Have Fun - Play With These Prompts By Adding More Keywords, Then

COMBINE WORDS – EXCHANGE WORDS & EVEN ADD YOUR OWN WORDS

I Recommend Checking The Prompt Number, Keeping A Record Of Those You've Tested

Number	SIMPLE PROMPT
1	Ancient Encounters
2	All Seeing Eye
3	Healing Waters
4	Lost Civilizations
5	Musical Codes
6	Monumental Structure
7	Remains Of A Dream
8	Land Before Time
9	Keys To The Past
10	Lush Vegetation
11	Prehistoric America
12	Festival Of Lights
13	Wild Animals Around Me
14	The Wooden Walls
15	Building Dreams
16	Symbols Of Heritage
17	The Will Of The Gods
18	Phenomenal Encounters
19	Center Of The Universe
20	Articles Of Delphi
21	Mysterious Discovery
22	Water Of Life
23	World Treasures
24	Around The World In 80 Days
25	To Kill A Mockingbird
26	Hakka Migration
27	Hedge Trimmer
28	Jupiter Ascending
29	Happy Smile

Number	SIMPLE PROMPT
30	Modern Craftsmanship
31	Crafting Flying Wonders
32	Hail The Conquering Hero
33	New Year's Eve
34	Complete Game Plan
35	Permaculture Principles
36	Two-Minute Warning
37	Soylent Green
38	Ab-Normal Beauty
39	Stand Up Guy
40	Mysterious Island
41	Tech & Innovation
42	Historical Animals
43	Butcher's Wife
44	Dancing Polka Ghosts
45	Johannesburg South Africa
46	Blue Birds
47	Great Summer Meadow
48	Jack Frost
49	Star Trek
50	Raisin In The Sun
51	Grass Is Greener
52	Borrowed Hearts
53	I Can See For Miles
54	Magic Kits
55	Rhinestone Cowboy
56	Drill For Oil
57	Quarterback Sneak
58	Golden Tripod

59	**Towering Inferno**
60	**Girl With The Dragon Tattoo**
61	**Don't Let The Sun Go Down**
62	**Watering Schedule**
63	**Rare Breed**
64	**Navigating History**
65	**Life Less Ordinary**
66	**Public Transportation Systems**
67	**Predator Requiem**
68	**Ghosts On The Loose**
69	**Golden Eye Finger**
70	**Femme Fatale**
71	**Daisy Bouquet**
72	**Mountain Men**
73	**Magical Watermelons**
74	**The Good Witch**
75	**Touching Wild Horses**
76	**The Omega Man**
77	**Trading Places**
78	**Amazing Adventures**
79	**Moonlight Moondance**
80	**Pinecone Adventure**
81	**Poppy Seed**
82	**Teen Wolf**
83	**Tomb Raiders**
84	**Breakfast Burritos**
85	**Food Sovereignty Movements**
86	**Hunger Games**
87	**Machine Learning Algorithm**
88	**Frame Of Mind**
89	**Music & Lyrics**
90	**Black Mask Deva**
91	**Incantation Chants**
92	**Enigmatic Ghost Ship**
93	**Nature-Based Therapy**
94	**Along The Santa Fe Trail**
95	**After The Sunset**
96	**Tomorrowland's Truths**

97	**A Great Big World**
98	**Condensed Milk**
99	**Bengal Brigade**
100	**The World Is Not Enough**
101	**Attention Spans**
102	**Goal Line Defense**
103	**The Train Robbers**
104	**Mystery Men**
105	**Cleats On My Shoes**
106	**Sheep In The Meadow**
107	**Floating Landscapes**
108	**Charcoal Pencil**
109	**Renaissance Period**
110	**Dirty Rotten Scoundrels**
111	**Governance Structures**
112	**Little Help**
113	**Secret Window**
114	**Decal Stickers**
115	**Devil Wears Prada**
116	**Galactic Cucumber Cowboy Rodeo**
117	**Lost Horizon**
118	**Reakfast Foods**
119	**Bee Movie**
120	**Ancient Lines Deciphered**
121	**Primary Colors**
122	**Dreaming Of Love**
123	**Running Lights**
124	**Poison Ivy**
125	**Hotel California**
126	**Total Recall**
127	**Out Of The Shadows**
128	**Cashew Ice Cream**
129	**Beasts In The Barnyard**
130	**One Lucky Elephant**
131	**Brand New Day**
132	**Bristle Feathers**
133	**Harsh Times**
134	**Secrets Of Delphi**

135	**Pragmatic Love**
136	**Baroque Art**
137	**Onion Rings**
138	**French Connection**
139	**Wonders Of The Old World**
140	**Indian English**
141	**Empty Soul**
142	**Navigating The Open Sea**
143	**Orphan Horse**
144	**Burning Daylight**
145	**Breach Of Contract**
146	**Potato Squad**
147	**Ghost In The House**
148	**Humanitarian Aid**
149	**Down Periscope**
150	**Mass Communication**
151	**Prehistoric Period**
152	**Beyond Christmas**
153	**Honey Nut Cheerios**
154	**Glaze Firing**
155	**Walk In The Sun**
156	**Elusive Butterfly**
157	**Antonov Ruslan**
158	**Space Tourism**
159	**Uno Moss**
160	**White Castle Burgers**
161	**Made For Christmas**
162	**Are We There Yet**
163	**Bone Carvings**
164	**Guess Who's Coming To Dinner**
165	**Show Jumping**
166	**Hold & Serve**
167	**Cutting Summer Grass**
168	**Canned Tuna**
169	**Ladybugs On My Flowers**
170	**Observe & Report**
171	**Country Girl**
172	**The Sky's On Fire**

173	**Sunflower Seeds**
174	**Written Correspondence**
175	**Wizard Of Oz**
176	**Amazing Grace**
177	**Batch Normalization**
178	**Genetic Algorithms**
179	**Safflower Oil**
180	**Baby On Board**
181	**Comedians On Stage**
182	**Friendship Is Forever**
183	**Shimmering Night Lights**
184	**Ancient Geoglyphs**
185	**Ernest Hemingway**
186	**On The Waterfront**
187	**Bangkok Thailand**
188	**Renewable Energy Systems**
189	**Drop Shot**
190	**Garden Of Eden**
191	**Dancing Or Eating Salsa**
192	**Company Men**
193	**Usual Suspects**
194	**Almost An Angel**
195	**One Million Years B.C.**
196	**Woodpecker Song**
197	**Mythical Creatures**
198	**Los Angeles United States**
199	**Picture Window**
200	**Two Week Notice**
201	**Discarded Textiles**
202	**Blue In The Face**
203	**Black Stallion**
204	**Sole Survivor**
205	**Chicken Parmesan**
206	**Dandelion Greens**
207	**Huffman Coding**
208	**Kidney Bean Salad**
209	**Collecting Antique Watches**
210	**Jungle Book Adventures**

211	Approaching The Unknown
212	Pearls In My Milk
213	History Of Experiments
214	East Of Eden
215	Last Starfighter
216	Tourch Singer
217	Fight Club
218	Thunder Road
219	Video Game Storytelling
220	Torn Curtain
221	Church Organ Pipes
222	Invisible Signs
223	Salmon Fishing In Yeman
224	Unsupervised Learning
225	No Easy Answers
226	Global Health Equity
227	Beautiful Pink Flowers
228	True Grit
229	Crop Circles
230	After The Thin Man
231	Arabian Nights
232	Beef Stroganoff
233	Once Upon A Time
234	Stairway To Heaven
235	Bioluminescent Plankton
236	The Bikini Machine
237	Twelve Angry Men
238	Predicting Tremors
239	Missing In Action
240	Canned Mushrooms
241	Water Polo
242	To Be Or Not To Be
243	Social Media Memories
244	Track & Field
245	Black-Eyed Peas
246	I Dig Rock & Roll Music
247	Field Hockey
248	Back To 1942
249	Kaleidoscopic Dreams
250	Collard Greens In My Teeth
251	Me Want Cookie
252	Peanut Butter Wizard Duel
253	Oklahoma Oklahoma City
254	Wearable Technology
255	Trapped In Paradise
256	Operation C.I.A.
257	Uncommon Whispering Winds
258	Leo Tolstoy
259	Poppy Seeds
260	All The Money In The World
261	Fresh Green Grass
262	White Sandy Beach
263	Juggling Finances
264	Frozen Fruits
265	Destry Rides Again
266	Down In The Valley
267	Star Spangle Girl
268	Natural Dyeing Techniques
269	It's Kind Of A Funny Story
270	Cello In My Jell-O
271	Shot In The Dark
272	Philosophy Of Technology
273	Home Energy Audits
274	Snows Of Kilmanjaro
275	The Coral Sea
276	After Earth
277	Unfinished Life
278	Sage Brush
279	Cognitive Dissonance Theory
280	Sum Of All Fears
281	Devil's Rejects
282	Role Of Problem-Solving
283	Water Guns
284	Hot Shots
285	Urban Green Management
286	Second Chances

287	Funky Whispering Winds
288	Ancient Fire-Making
289	The Terminal
290	Rosé Vineyards
291	Frozen Soups
292	Chimichurri Sauce
293	Hybrid Bikes
294	Traditional Artistic Expressions
295	Happy Ever After
296	Pancake Detective Agency
297	Leap Of Faith
298	Happy Little Girl
299	Expressive Arts Therapy
300	Sacred Tombs
301	Penalty Kill
302	Black Magic Woman
303	Traditional Culinary Arts
304	Fox & The Child
305	Environmental Activism
306	My Science Project
307	Empire Strikes Back
308	Cold Mountain
309	Alien Uprising
310	Feedforward Neural Networks
311	My Dear Clemetine
312	State Of Play
313	Little Shop Of Horrors
314	Lazarus Papers
315	Beverly Hills Mansion
316	Empty Vessel
317	Guidance Systems
318	Searching Algorithms
319	Pretty Woman
320	Revolving Door
321	Modern Standard Arabic
322	Nick Of Time
323	Vinyl Record Collecting
324	Frozen Dinners

325	Wisdom Restoration
326	Whipped Cream
327	Most Wanted
328	American Football
329	Employee Of The Month
330	Historical Mysteries
331	Flip Flops
332	Hungry Outsiders
333	Media & Entertainment
334	Catch Me A Spy
335	Long Train Running
336	Return Of The King
337	Balcony Gardening
338	Google Chrome
339	Lost Cause
340	Live & Let Die
341	Canned Soups
342	Runoff Election
343	Miniature Painting
344	Judgment Day
345	Delaware Dover
346	Jurassic Park
347	Big Brown Eyes
348	Crazy Rich Asians
349	Watermelon Spaceship Odyssey
350	Radix Sort
351	You're Gonna Need A Bigger Boat
352	Open-Heart Surgery
353	Dress Shirts
354	Before They Hatch
355	Silver Bells
356	Silent Voice
357	Mysterious Pancake Wizard Duel
358	Ghost Protocol
359	Simple Plan
360	Sitar Artists
361	Ancient Rocks
362	Rally Around The Flag

363	**Condiments & Sauces**
364	**Recurrent Neural Networks**
365	**Shanghai Noon**
366	**Marker Fragments**
367	**Boogie Woogie**
368	**Like A Rolling Stone**
369	**Ethics Of Ai**
370	**Goodbye Mama**
371	**Kia Optima**
372	**The Art Of Bonsai**
373	**Endangered Languages**
374	**Alaska Juneau**
375	**Laptop Mystery**
376	**Natural Cleaning Solutions**
377	**Just Getting Started**
378	**Oddly Shaped Clouds**
379	**Urban Well-Being**
380	**Radiation Fog**
381	**City Of Oz**
382	**Peasantry Castle**
383	**Juggling Work & Play**
384	**Peacock Fern**
385	**Puppy Love**
386	**Endless Summer**
387	**Hong Kong China**
388	**Strangers When We Meet**
389	**Megacity Challenges**
390	**Tail Feathers**
391	**Natural Remedies**
392	**Birth Of A Nation**
393	**Brass Teapot**
394	**On Moonlight Bay**
395	**Global Access**
396	**The Future Of Work**
397	**Youth Environmental Programs**
398	**Parisian French**
399	**Fuzzy Logic**
400	**The Postman**

401	**Grandpa For Chistmas**
402	**Devil's Tomb**
403	**Pride Of The Yankees**
404	**Change Up**
405	**Role Of Synchronicity**
406	**Boney Maroney**
407	**Savory Pies**
408	**Iced Coffee**
409	**Dragon Fruit**
410	**All Night Long**
411	**To Infinity & Beyond**
412	**Smashing Pumpkins**
413	**Brass Bottle**
414	**Markov Decision Processes**
415	**Gene Editing Technology**
416	**Doll Accessories**
417	**Speech-Language Pathologist**
418	**Soy Milk-Based Ice Cream**
419	**Transforming Microbes**
420	**Distinquished Gentleman**
421	**Providing Sanctuary**
422	**Play-Action Pass**
423	**Legal Services**
424	**Cognitive Development**
425	**Fermented Fruits**
426	**Banana Peels**
427	**Dime Defense**
428	**Unusual Shimmering Specters**
429	**Penny Serenade**
430	**Balloon Stomp**
431	**Angels & Demons**
432	**Back Up Plan**
433	**Gathering Of Woman**
434	**Sing Sing A Song**
435	**Great Buck Howard**
436	**A Whiter Shade Of Pale**
437	**Hornet's Nest**
438	**Martial Arts**

439	Garden Fork
440	Australian English
441	Time For Public Services
442	Clear & Present Danger
443	Cat Ballou
444	Bridge To Nowhere
445	Cow's Milk
446	Trail Mix
447	Dress Shoes
448	Labyrinth Maze
449	Thirsty Lips
450	Strange Floating Islands
451	One Night Stand
452	Sweet Potato
453	Mobile Technology
454	Out Of Time
455	Fruit Slices
456	Carpet Ride
457	Shadow Wolves
458	Indiana Indianapolis Speedway
459	Vines & Creepers
460	Some Like It Hot
461	Kentucky Frankfort
462	Catch Me If You Can
463	American Buffalo
464	Chirping Crickets
465	Body Language
466	The Sea Wolves
467	Gliding Shimmering Stars
468	Holiday Inn
469	Shawshank Redemption
470	Allen Bolt
471	Connect Four
472	Sushi Rolls
473	The Outpost
474	Four Square
475	Starting Pitcher
476	Evaporated Milk

477	Tomb Of Dragon Emperor
478	Martian Child
479	Taking Care Of Business
480	Nurturing Botanical Marvels
481	The Frozen Front
482	Image Processing Algorithms
483	Night Shift
484	Savoring Diverse Flavors
485	Lonely Boy
486	Frost Date
487	See No Evil Hear No Evil
488	Tulip Blossoms
489	Image Creation
490	The Secret Service
491	Software Development
492	Purple Rose Of Cairo
493	Sitting On The Dock
494	Herbal Medicine
495	Laughter Yoga
496	For Your Consideration
497	Out Of Sight
498	Pasta Dishes
499	This Property Is Condemned
500	Know Thyself
501	Cinderella Story
502	Frozen Breakfast Bowls
503	Science Of Happiness Studies
504	Man Overboard
505	Law Of Attraction
506	Rhode Island Providence
507	Bottle Rocket
508	Red Dawn
509	Outrageous Fortune
510	Girl Who Kicked The Hornet's Nest
511	Transom Window
512	Silent Running
513	Harnessing Nature's Power
514	Crouching Tiger Hidden Dragon

515	**Trouble With Angels**
516	**Conquering Heights**
517	**Autumn Leaves**
518	**Bizarre Doughnuts**
519	**Campaign Finance**
520	**Echoing Laughter**
521	**Online Shopping**
522	**Unknown Love**
523	**Radio Beacon**
524	**Across The Universe**
525	**Electric Guitar**
526	**Coconut Oil**
527	**Bounty Hunter**
528	**Broken Flowers**
529	**Open Door**
530	**Performance Poetry**
531	**Empty Gaze**
532	**Zenith Terraria**
533	**Greening Concrete Jungles**
534	**Nutmeg Aroma**
535	**Farming Practices**
536	**Searching For The Future**
537	**Supervised Learning**
538	**Tepary Tuxedos**
539	**Wraps For Warmth**
540	**Electric Bikes**
541	**Digging Bar**
542	**Animal Rights Activism**
543	**Hidden Lake**
544	**Toggle Dancing Bolts**
545	**Instant Oats**
546	**Parental Guidance**
547	**Medical Technology**
548	**Witness For Love**
549	**Pesto Sauce Art**
550	**False Start**
551	**Digital Literacy**
552	**Three Coins In A Fountain**

553	**Pizza Superhero Showdown**
554	**Man Eating Fire**
555	**Textile Art**
556	**Blue Summer Ocean**
557	**Troll Hunters**
558	**Once In A Lifetime**
559	**Prose Poetry**
560	**Ancient Period**
561	**Role Of Coincidence**
562	**They Arrived**
563	**Interventions For Well-Being**
564	**Observational Astronomy**
565	**Beauty Shop**
566	**Caraway Seeds**
567	**Bright Summer Sky**
568	**The Real Mccoy**
569	**Energy Beings**
570	**Just Married**
571	**Missile Toe**
572	**Shape Of Water**
573	**Happy Feet Dancing**
574	**Lucky Success**
575	**Trial & Error**
576	**Steam Fog**
577	**House Of Dracula**
578	**Big Trees**
579	**The Voyage Home**
580	**Leadership In Conservation**
581	**Breakfast Club**
582	**Road Warrior**
583	**Apple Juice Harvest**
584	**Distant Horizon**
585	**American Violet**
586	**Where Legends Begin**
587	**Empty Space**
588	**Istanbul Turkey**
589	**Kiss Of The Dragon**
590	**Secrets Behind Windows**

591	Unusual Shimmering Stars
592	Massachusetts Hills
593	Havarti Cheese Festival
594	Minimalist Lifestyle Practices
595	Aloe Vera Plantation
596	Byzantine Art
597	Historical Fiction
598	Deep Impact
599	Happy Trails To You
600	Soccer Ball
601	Fromage Blanc
602	Hat Trick
603	Bullpen Session
604	Role Of Folklore In Identity
605	Tokyo Skyline
606	Graphic Algorithms
607	Reading Bedtime Stories
608	Roque One
609	Straight Talk
610	Ebook Technology
611	Musical Chairs
612	Homeland Security
613	Last Emperor
614	Tofu Scramble
615	Fashion Upcycling Projects
616	Vertical Gardening
617	Wide Receiver
618	Dangerous Crossing
619	General Aviation
620	Gardening Projects
621	King Of Kings
622	Twelve O'Clock High
623	Dark Side Of The Moon
624	History Of The World
625	Blocking Traffic
626	Road Potholes
627	Lifeboat Lightkeepers
628	Conformity Phenomena

629	Old Yeller
630	Swiss Cheese On The Moon
631	Mojave Moon
632	Radiating Time
633	Social Relationships
634	Entertaining With Humor
635	That Evening Sun
636	Face Masks Requirred
637	The Music Man
638	The Producers
639	Nothing In Common
640	Going My Way
641	Nature-Inspired Design
642	Jellyfish Monster
643	Deep Space Exploration
644	Distant Shores
645	Narrative Poetry
646	Attention Mechanism
647	Penguins Of Madagascar
648	Hidden Valley
649	Dark Tower
650	Golf Lessons
651	Frankly My Dear
652	Ides Of March
653	Back Roads
654	Heap Sort
655	Root System
656	I Am Your Father
657	King Of Hollywood
658	Advise & Consent
659	Here We Go Again
660	Matrix Reloaded
661	Cranberry Spritzer
662	Construction & Engineering
663	Sustainable Living
664	Veterinary Technician
665	Teacher's Pet
666	Little Mermaid

667	Loch Ness Monster
668	Running Mates
669	Dreams Of Dancing Shadows
670	A Star Is Born
671	Pillow Talk
672	Scrimshaw Carvings
673	Career Opportunities
674	Hidden Truth
675	Pin-Up Girl
676	Don't Call Me Shirley
677	Clothing Workshops
678	Research & Development
679	Drum Set
680	Hustle & Heat
681	Flying Leathernecks
682	Lost Roanoke Colony
683	Hemp Seed Oil
684	You Are The One
685	Final Destination
686	Raging Bull
687	Automotive Technician
688	Semiplume Feathers
689	English Muffins
690	Intermittent Fasting
691	Seaweed Snacks
692	Sporting Events
693	Household Plants
694	Eurofighter Typhoon
695	Gin Rummy For My Tummy
696	I Will Always Love You
697	Summer Weather
698	Quiet Night
699	Dark Waters
700	Friendly Persuasion
701	X-Ray Machine
702	Time Heals All Wounds
703	There Goes The Bride
704	Conflict Resolution

705	Witness Protection
706	Moth Beans
707	Bizarre Cowboy Circus
708	Hide & Seek
709	Tops & Bottoms
710	Lily Pond
711	Howdy Doody
712	Out Of The Woods
713	Human Enhancements
714	Robo Cop
715	Fluffy Marshmallow Treasures
716	Voltage Regulator
717	Empty Nest
718	Jazz Singer
719	Midsummer Night's Dream
720	Just Like Teen Spirit
721	Pecan Pie
722	I'll See You In My Dreams
723	Pitch Black
724	Deep Ecology
725	Swing High Swing Low
726	Moving Mountains
727	Lemon Trees
728	Dirty Laundry
729	Still Waters
730	Crazy Stupid Love
731	Blue Crush
732	Temple Of Dome
733	He Meaning Of Life
734	Last Airbender
735	Don't Make Waves
736	A Sailor's Journey
737	Break Up
738	You Had Me At Hello
739	Almond Yogurt
740	Chill Out Mama
741	Dizzy Floating Orbs
742	Prancer Returns

743	Jean-Jacques Rousseau
744	Chocolate Chip Cookies
745	Social Relationships
746	Gourmet Cooking
747	Reinforcement Learning
748	Primary Love
749	Equality In Stem Fields
750	Aegis Of The Universe
751	Practices In Forestry
752	Daddy Day Care
753	Slippery Rocks
754	Sun Spots
755	Mysterious Triangle Debunked
756	Pillow Fight
757	Moscow Architecture
758	Magical Mystery Tour
759	Quick & The Dead
760	Rubik's Cube
761	The Amazing Adventure
762	Ace In Hand
763	Message In A Bottle
764	Phantom Menace
765	Constantine The Great
766	Pace Colonization
767	Ethics Of Artificial Intelligence
768	Bachelor Party
769	Chocolate Fondue Rivers
770	The Rapture
771	Environmental Education
772	Cocoa Puffs
773	Impact Of Urban Farming
774	Blades Of Glory
775	Beautiful Models
776	Peanut Oil
777	Two Way Stretch
778	Symbolism Of Colors
779	Infinite Worlds Of Love
780	Holding Court
781	Perfect Game
782	Documenting Narratives
783	Existentialism In Literature
784	Milking Cows
785	Warm Summer Air
786	Salsa Dancing
787	Software Developer
788	Bass Drum
789	Pride & Glory
790	Thick As Thieves
791	Going Overboard
792	Bypass Grafting
793	Our Lips Are Sealed
794	The Odd Couple
795	Battle Force
796	Gravel Bikes
797	Intrapersonal Communication
798	I Love You More
799	Enjoying The Shade Of Trees
800	Brussels Sprouts
801	New Kid In Town
802	Desert Fox
803	Jet Cockpit
804	Return To Me
805	Regional Aircraft
806	Music Within
807	Organic Gardening Classes
808	Penny Saved Penny Earned
809	Mri Machine
810	Pocket Squares
811	Women Writers Working
812	The Digital Age
813	Ghost Rider
814	Boeing Dreamliner
815	No Scoring At All
816	Rights & Climate Change
817	Peter Pan
818	Motorcycle Diaries

819	Frosted Flakes
820	Errand Boy
821	Hot Chili Powder
822	Angel Heart
823	Connecting With Frequencies
824	Cat's Playing Poker
825	Big Miracle
826	Light Emitting Diode
827	Center Of All Things
828	Potato Robot Rebellion
829	Glowing Jellyfish
830	Ghost Writer
831	Cryptographic Algorithms
832	Mechanic Resurrection
833	League Of Their Own
834	Boeing Boeing
835	High Spirits
836	Almond Ice Cream
837	Adventures In Babysitting
838	Singing Sand Dunes
839	Search For The Holy Grail
840	On A Clear Day
841	Jealous Window Shades
842	Polling Data
843	Democracy & Governance
844	Particle Swarm Optimization
845	Dahlia Blossoms
846	Water Balloons
847	Opportunity Knocks
848	Night Sky
849	American Dreamer
850	Mullholland Drive Landscape
851	Blonde Ambition
852	Hyacinth Beans
853	Electronic Instruments
854	Triple Play
855	Fenugreek Seeds
856	Source Code

857	Oh My God
858	Body Language
859	Ground Ball
860	Big Business
861	Hope & Glory
862	Beacon Hill
863	Alternative Consciousness
864	The Principal
865	Beautiful Day In The Neighborhood
866	I Dreamed There Was No War
867	Shanghai Nights
868	Order Of The Phoenix
869	Renewable Energy Sources
870	Go Ahead Make My Day
871	Quirky Hoedown
872	Taxi Driver
873	Simulated Annealing
874	Hare’s Breath
875	North To Alaska
876	End Of The Road
877	Rock My World
878	Lima Beans
879	Cat's Cradle
880	The Gang's All Here
881	Pan's Flute
882	Environmental Ethics
883	Parallel Universes
884	Random Harvest
885	Battle Hymn
886	In Wonderland
887	Freedom Ride
888	Pruning Shears For Hair
889	Learning To Fly
890	Endless Ocean
891	Talk Of The Town
892	Pucker Pepper Pickles
893	Billy's Jelly Beans
894	Boyfriend For Christmas

895	Sky Captain
896	Fortune Cookie
897	Come Sail Away
898	Lincoln's Last Moment
899	Artificial Emotional Intelligence
900	Mastering Discipline
901	Moon Over Parador
902	How Sweet It Is
903	Blade Runner
904	Environmental Cleanups
905	Porsche Panamera
906	Cosmic Wizard Duel
907	Wizard Spells
908	Stone Temples
909	Bummer Morning Blues
910	The Garden Of Eden
911	Fear & Phobias
912	Keen Eyes Of Green
913	Augmented Reality
914	A Dog's Tale
915	Bucket Solution
916	Recycled Paper Creatively
917	Competitive Chess
918	Canned Vegetables
919	Wet-On-Wet Technique
920	Continental Divide
921	Advanced Encryption Standard
922	Blind Man's Bluff
923	Small Time Crooks
924	Striking Distance
925	North Dakota Bismarck
926	Urban Composting
927	Constellation Scorpius
928	Solar Panels
929	Social Impact Of Video Games
930	Missing In America
931	Color Therapy
932	It Happened At The World's Fair

933	Cross Of Iron
934	Last Man Standing
935	Australian Shepherd
936	Sustainable Water Management
937	Swatting Infield Flies
938	Our Early Descendants
939	Aztec Calendar
940	Bright Sunny Morning
941	Virtual Reality Headset
942	Hawaii Honolulu
943	Whiskey History
944	Remember The Titans
945	Burning Passion
946	Angel On My Shoulder
947	Triangle Clarified
948	Unemployment Solutions
949	Phantom Of The Opera
950	History Of Traditional Remedies
951	Let The Sunshine In
952	Jane Austen
953	African Villages
954	Rocky Roads
955	Computer Technology
956	Peanut Butter
957	Blue Summer Sky
958	Medical Assistant
959	The Rainmaker
960	Lawn Mower
961	Endless Road
962	Wisdom & Sustainability
963	Kitchen Technology
964	Brown Bat
965	Preccious Pretzel Adventure
966	Dark Crystal
967	Phone Booth
968	Funny Face
969	Canola Oil
970	The Runaway Jury

971	Shredded Wheat
972	The Out Of Towners
973	Africa Screams
974	Bright Shining Star
975	Bat Cave
976	Essential Oils
977	Fashion Practices
978	Ancient Greek Philosophy
979	Cosmic Pizza Wizard Spells
980	Zone Coverage
981	German U-Boat
982	Coconut Yogurt
983	Prehistoric Monuments
984	Colorful Gel Pens
985	Legend Of Tarzan
986	Appropriation vs Appreciation
987	Hot Air Ballooning
988	Funny Lady
989	Blackjack Table
990	Emotional Intelligence
991	Doughnut Ninja Academy
992	The Right Stuff
993	Defiant Ones
994	The Peacemakers
995	Shea Butter Sunburn
996	Empty Promises
997	Princess & The Pirate
998	Canned Fruits
999	Future Of Bioengineering
1000	Significance Of Music
1001	Pampas Grass
1002	Clear Summer Sky
1003	No Man's Land
1004	Urban Beekeeping
1005	Beyond The Reach
1006	Nickel Defense
1007	Forest Management
1008	Kindergarten Cop

1009	Ice Station Zebra
1010	Seven Years In Tibet
1011	French Horn
1012	Living Expos
1013	Homo Sapiens
1014	Chocolate Mousse
1015	Autonomous Systems
1016	Black Widow
1017	Quiet Summer Afternoon
1018	Resident Evil
1019	Collateral Loan
1020	Kids' Bikes
1021	Stand By For Action
1022	Winter Wind
1023	Count Of Monte Cristo
1024	Body Of Evidence
1025	Animal Kingdom
1026	Rare Talking Parrots
1027	America's Sweethearts
1028	Funny People
1029	Grande Ecole
1030	To Be A Millionaire
1031	Transportation & Logistics
1032	Aquatic Plants
1033	Effects Of Music
1034	Pancake Superhero Showdown
1035	Wild Rice
1036	Bridge Of Spies
1037	If I Didn't Care
1038	It's Great Feeling
1039	Endangered Animal Species
1040	In Time
1041	Barbarian Invasions
1042	Morning Glory
1043	Queen Of The Desert
1044	Imaging Technology
1045	Hidden Figures
1046	You Are My Heart

1047	Coconut Water
1048	Tour Of Duty In Iraq
1049	Hidden Identity
1050	Effects Of Social Isolation
1051	Bringing Down The House
1052	Just Got Paid
1053	Horrible Bosses
1054	Christmas Carol
1055	Neuroscience Of Creativity
1056	Between Heaven & Hell
1057	Mind-Body Connection
1058	Integrated Circuit
1059	Blue Cheese
1060	Nearest Neighbors
1061	Flange Nuts
1062	Snare Drums
1063	Double Dutch
1064	Yardlong Beans
1065	Urban Rooftop Initiatives
1066	Sleepy Time
1067	Not My Forte
1068	Stomp The Yard
1069	Fruit Skewers
1070	Ranch Dressing
1071	Flags Of Our Father
1072	Rolling Hills
1073	Quantum Of Solace
1074	Ghostly Ogre
1075	Rare Floating Islands
1076	Brazilian Portuguese
1077	Languages Revitalization
1078	Band Of Brothers
1079	Dynamics Analysis
1080	Staple Gun
1081	Coconut Butter Cookies
1082	Funny Money
1083	High In The Syhawk
1084	Tall Green Grass

1085	Diamonds Are Forever
1086	Reason & Control
1087	Worm Armageddon
1088	Mission Impossible
1089	Girl Next Door
1090	Peppermint Fields
1091	Cast A Giant Shadow
1092	Bermuda Triangle
1093	Ghosts Of Girlfriends Past
1094	Model Ship Building
1095	Match Point
1096	Pastoral Poetry
1097	Thunder In Paradise
1098	Forces Of Nature
1099	Continental Philosophy
1100	Divine Guidance
1101	Energy Production Methods
1102	Spy Who Loved Me
1103	Whiter Shade Of Pale
1104	Tuba Rock Band
1105	Little Bit Of Heaven
1106	Standard Russian
1107	Fire-Resistant Clothing
1108	Ghost & The Darkness
1109	Shining Light
1110	Power Play
1111	Falling Summer Leaves
1112	Ricotta Cheese
1113	Quinoa Porridge
1114	Rainbow Dreams
1115	Big Trouble
1116	Singin' In Rain
1117	Still Water Runs Deep
1118	Satellite Galaxy
1119	Fruit Bats
1120	Human Nature
1121	Bow Light
1122	Radio Flyer

1123	Multiplicity Wonders
1124	Volkswagen Atlas
1125	Great Balls Of Fire
1126	Gingerbread Man
1127	Jack Of All Trades
1128	Yellow Lentils
1129	Lentil-Based Meat
1130	Eagle Has Landed
1131	Alien Attack
1132	Stormy Monday
1133	Across The Line
1134	Thundering Rain
1135	Secrets Of The Mountain
1136	Girls Just Want To Have Fun
1137	A New Hope
1138	Queen Of The Damned
1139	There Was A Crooked Man
1140	Lovely Shimmering Waters
1141	Mental Health
1142	Butter Me Up
1143	Support Your Local Sheriff
1144	Early Morning Sun
1145	Insertion Sort
1146	Love Conquers All
1147	I See Dead People
1148	Hard To Kill
1149	Divine Inspiration
1150	Swiss German
1151	Colorful Glowing Fireflies
1152	Fantasy Of The Mind
1153	On Borrowed Time
1154	National Velvet
1155	Bayesian Networks
1156	No More Suppression
1157	Dancing Shadows
1158	Unbearable Lightness
1159	Bustin' Loose
1160	Falling Leaves

1161	Peanut Sauce
1162	Flying Fox
1163	Back Door To Hell
1164	Cognitive Computing
1165	Ancient Water Conservation
1166	Rosetta Stone
1167	Apocalypse Now
1168	Finance & Banking
1169	Romantic Comedy
1170	Recycled Materials In Home Decor
1171	Smokey & The Banditr
1172	Land Management
1173	Mixed Martial Arts
1174	Ash To Ash
1175	Anniversay Party
1176	Heuristic Search
1177	Bright Morning Sun
1178	Whimsical Unicorn Journey
1179	Anchors Aweigh
1180	Energy Drinks
1181	Secret Life Of Bees
1182	Apple For The Teacher
1183	Planning & Design
1184	Other Instruments
1185	Life With Father
1186	Social Media On Education
1187	New Kind Of Love
1188	Renewable Energy
1189	Toy Instruments
1190	Deed Goes To Town
1191	Never A Dull Moment
1192	Sleepless In Seattle
1193	Bike-Powered Energy Systems
1194	Rice Cakes With Toppings
1195	First Knight
1196	Deep Dark Forest
1197	Proud Zulu Nation
1198	Perfect Sense

1199	Role Of Luck In History
1200	Dreamy Dreamweaver
1201	Mixed Doubles
1202	South Dakota Pierre
1203	Two For The Road
1204	Nowhere In Africa
1205	Significant Indigenous Body Art
1206	Lord Of The Rings
1207	Curtain Pajamas
1208	Common Items
1209	Pickle Wizard Duel
1210	Dead Men Tell No Tales
1211	Thick Heads Collide
1212	Architecture Urban Planning
1213	Behind Blue Eyes
1214	Cold Winter Season
1215	Super Hornets
1216	Easy Virtue
1217	Fire Alarm
1218	It Happened On 5th Avenue
1219	Aquatic Aliens
1220	I'll Be Back
1221	The Sliver Fleet
1222	Behind The Garage Door
1223	Color Purple
1224	Old Lace
1225	Dimensions In Time
1226	Fava Beans
1227	Two Weak To Talk
1228	Drafting Table
1229	Zoysia Grass
1230	Fair Game
1231	Space Cowboys
1232	Cold Winter Evening
1233	Business Jets
1234	Digital Art
1235	Rake In The Money
1236	Giddy Singing Birds

1237	Cultural Revitalization Programs
1238	Lockheed Hercules
1239	Computer Interaction Interfaces
1240	Social Media On Friendships
1241	Operation Endgame
1242	Red Riding Hood
1243	Fermented Foods
1244	Model Airplane Building
1245	Walking Dead
1246	Run Silent Run Deep
1247	Balloon Keep Up
1248	Canned Chicken
1249	Osaka Japan
1250	Golden Child
1251	Caddy Shack
1252	Fescue Grass
1253	Iron Man Marathon
1254	Failure To Launch
1255	Explored Scientifically
1256	Potato Wedges
1257	Northern Skies
1258	Track Cycling
1259	Hidden Doors
1260	Oromo Tribe Village
1261	Social Comparison Phenomena
1262	Great Poetry
1263	Pretzel Spell
1264	Live Another Day
1265	Land Rights & Conservation
1266	Angel Food Cake
1267	Can’t Stop Dancing
1268	High School Musical
1269	Vise Grip Mystery
1270	Holiday In The Sun
1271	Job's Tears
1272	Empty Room
1273	Prosthetic Technology
1274	Rare Butterfly Wings

1275	My Fellow Americans
1276	Mysteries Of Antimatter
1277	Strategic Air Command
1278	Artistic Freedom & Censorship
1279	None But The Brave
1280	Cabin Fever
1281	Run-Length Encoding
1282	Great Escape
1283	Bi-Fold Doors
1284	The Old Man & The Sea
1285	Endless Desert
1286	Garlic Bread
1287	Bizarre Rebellion
1288	Pay The Ghost
1289	Out Cold
1290	Agape Love
1291	Perspectives On Sustainability
1292	The Runaway Train
1293	American Hustle
1294	Letterpress Printing
1295	Cream Of The Crop
1296	Black Rain
1297	Frontier Marshall
1298	Swing Dancing
1299	Den Of Thieves
1300	Blind Date
1301	Angel Has Fallen
1302	High & The Mighty
1303	Wuhan China
1304	Cap'n Crunch
1305	Natural Building Workshops
1306	Born Romantic
1307	Office Space
1308	New York City
1309	Black Sea
1310	Colonial Languages
1311	Celestine Prophecy
1312	Flightless Birds

1313	Electoral College
1314	Murphy's Romance
1315	Advection Fog
1316	Math Manipulatives
1317	In The Movies
1318	Under Siege
1319	Variational Autoencoders
1320	Book Club
1321	Water Toys
1322	Mutiny On The Bounty
1323	I Only Have Eyes For You
1324	Scarlet Runner Beans
1325	Natural Insect Repellents
1326	Frog Leg Competition
1327	The Ten Commandments
1328	Morning Birds
1329	Mound Builders
1330	Hell Is For Heroes
1331	Cruiser Bikes
1332	Man Of The Century
1333	Monuments Men
1334	Rumor Has It
1335	Devil May Care
1336	Cold Breakfast Cereals
1337	Night Vision Goggles
1338	Away We Go
1339	Meditation For Stress Relief
1340	Goodbye Stranger
1341	Pay It Forward
1342	Undercover Blues
1343	Keep Your Enemies Closer
1344	Bohemian Rhapsody
1345	Role Models
1346	Didactic Poetry
1347	Traditional Medicine
1348	Dawn Of Justice
1349	Bread Pudding
1350	You Talking To Me

1351	Oregon's Sunsets
1352	Contour Feathers
1353	Mexican Spanish
1354	OZ The Great & Powerful
1355	Slip Casting
1356	Consciousness Studies
1357	Deadly Impact
1358	Keys To The Kingdom
1359	Her Shimmering Specters
1360	Swimming Pool
1361	Forced Out Into The Open
1362	Cosmic Pizza Detective Mystery
1363	Shoulder Bags
1364	Doodling For Adults
1365	Spaceship Invasion
1366	Running On Empty
1367	Jet Power
1368	Horse Racing
1369	Quiet Summer Day
1370	Here Comes The Sun
1371	Hairy Adventures
1372	Identifying Avian Species
1373	Krill & Baleen Whales
1374	Real Life
1375	Birds Of A Feather Flock Together
1376	Hidden Forest
1377	Bell Book & Candle
1378	Rights & Environmental Justice
1379	Winter Snowstorm
1380	Deep Sea
1381	Geo Hunting Treasures
1382	Mexican Border Patrols
1383	Foul Play
1384	Clash Of The Titans
1385	Cowboy Circus
1386	Foaming Glowing Crystals
1387	Fallen On Broken Wings
1388	Quiet Evening Sunset

1389	Stars At War
1390	Hidden Gems
1391	One For The Money
1392	Field Of Yellow Sunflowers
1393	Gabriel García Márquez
1394	Fiddler On The Roof
1395	Grapeseed Oil
1396	Amateur Radio Operation
1397	Princess & The Warrior
1398	Outdoor Play Equipment
1399	Bridge On The River Kwai
1400	Spending Time Outdoors
1401	Paper Man
1402	Jalapeno Poppers
1403	California Sacramento
1404	Tzatziki Sauce
1405	Base Hit
1406	Container Gardens
1407	Changing Lanes
1408	Castle Keep
1409	I'm Off To Yokohama
1410	Transportation Solutions
1411	Arizona Phoenix
1412	Inherit The Wind
1413	Maine Augusta
1414	View To Kill
1415	Great Dictator
1416	Hungry Hungry Hippos
1417	Enchanted Unicorn
1418	Iowa Des Moines
1419	Irregular Galaxy
1420	Cottage Cheese
1421	Mother May I
1422	Secret Of My Success
1423	Exploring Celestial Bodies
1424	Against The Dark
1425	Captain From Castile
1426	Grafting Trees

1427	Age Of Heros
1428	Dream Team
1429	Funny About Love
1430	Butternut Squash
1431	Sacrifice Bunt
1432	Burning Love
1433	Broken Mirror
1434	High Noon
1435	Impact Of Biodiversity
1436	Ford Mustang
1437	Dream A Little Draam Of Me
1438	Lose A Guy In 10 Days
1439	Ceremonial Mounds
1440	Human Brain
1441	Empathy In Leadership
1442	Navy Beans
1443	Penguin Cowboy
1444	It's Wonderful Life
1445	Wildflower Field
1446	Knees The Bees
1447	Nature Immersion
1448	Falling In Love
1449	Five Corners
1450	The Scorpion King
1451	Black Pepper
1452	Optimization Algorithms
1453	Counterfeit Trailor
1454	Hocus Pocus
1455	Sweet Caroline
1456	Living Prophecies
1457	Expressions Through Color
1458	For Few Dollars More
1459	The Secret Agent
1460	Born To Run
1461	Green Rooftops
1462	West Virginia Mountains
1463	Snakes On The Plane
1464	High Anxiety

1465	Spies Like Us
1466	Mini Tacos
1467	Snacks & Finger Foods
1468	Indigenous Conservation
1469	In Your Eyes
1470	Here's Looking At You Kid
1471	Escaped From The Zoo
1472	Maker Communities
1473	Footloose & Fancy Free
1474	No Skin Off My Nose
1475	Belly Dancers
1476	Trolls In Your Garden
1477	Two Wrongs Don't Mright
1478	Sacrifice Fly
1479	Figure Skating
1480	Must Love Dogs
1481	Double Your Pleasure
1482	The Voynich Manuscript
1483	Earth Song
1484	Landscape Architecture
1485	Jack & The Beanstalk
1486	Lehenga Cholis
1487	Traditional Healing Methods
1488	Vise Versa
1489	Son Of God
1490	Little Black Book
1491	Double Jeopardy
1492	Lockheed Martin Raptor
1493	Train To Santa Fe
1494	Anomaly Detection
1495	Bad Boys
1496	Beef Fat
1497	Batting Average
1498	Against All Odds
1499	Fox Spirit
1500	Here Come The Waves
1501	Kindness & Generosity
1502	Perspectives On Climate Change

1503	Cross Creek
1504	Back In The U.S.
1505	Beyond The Sea
1506	Nut-Based Spreads
1507	Living In Material World
1508	Petrarchan Sonnet
1509	Red Autumn Leaves
1510	Grace & Skill
1511	Funny Girl
1512	Restoration Efforts
1513	Doll Furniture
1514	Houston We Have A Problem
1515	Limestone Village
1516	Frankenstein Meets Wolf Man
1517	Broken Glass Everywhere
1518	Going The Distance
1519	Pretzel Robot Rebellion
1520	Unlikely Angel
1521	Game Plan
1522	Logistic Regression
1523	The Ninth Gate
1524	Fire Shelter
1525	Thermal Imaging Camera
1526	Conspiracy Theories
1527	Raku Kiln-Fire Pottery
1528	Don't Cry For Me Argentina
1529	Romance Rebellion
1530	Science & Spirituality
1531	Art Therapy Trauma Recovery
1532	Mend A Broken Heart
1533	Zest For Life
1534	Lightning In Bottle
1535	Social Media On Body Imaging
1536	Kiln-Washed Pottery
1537	Flight Of The Navigator
1538	Golden Summer Evening
1539	Dancing Fireflies
1540	Crossbody Bags
1541	Folklore & Mythology
1542	Truth Doctrines
1543	Disorderly Orderly
1544	Memiors Of A Geisha
1545	Home For Christmas
1546	Sponge Painting
1547	The Never Ending Story
1548	Zany Pancake Ninja Party
1549	Herbal Medicine Preservation
1550	Canned Pumpkin
1551	Blue Line
1552	Mindful Rewards
1553	Toy Robots
1554	That Thing You Do
1555	Speed Skating
1556	Chicken Run
1557	Saguaro Cactus
1558	Nocturnal Animals Hunting
1559	Performing Arts
1560	Striving For Eco-Conservation
1561	Independent Candidate
1562	Coconut Oil-Based Butter
1563	Alexander The Great
1564	Endless Blue Sky
1565	Nanny For Christmas
1566	I Write The Love Songs
1567	Lego Building Challenges
1568	Folklore & Oral Tradition Studies
1569	Model Rocketry
1570	Friends With Benefits
1571	Lablab Beans
1572	Kick The Can
1573	Baked Goods
1574	Urban Gardening
1575	Education & E-Learning
1576	Red Ripe Apple
1577	Digital Communication
1578	Natural Hair Care

1579	On The Reviera
1580	Gardening For Urban Dwellers
1581	King Solomon's Mines
1582	Sign Language
1583	Reservoir Dogs
1584	Chalk Paintings
1585	Educational Toys
1586	Preserving Musical Heritage
1587	Barrel Cactus
1588	Batteries Not Included
1589	Canny Edge Detection
1590	Mummy & Daddy
1591	Slumdog Millionaire
1592	Bird On A Wire
1593	Dueling With Finesse
1594	It's Complicated
1595	Orchard Planting
1596	Casino Royale
1597	Knight & Day
1598	Silent Guardian
1599	Waste Recycling
1600	Urban Homesteading
1601	Goes To College
1602	Basic Income Debates
1603	Promoting Social Cohesion
1604	Frozen Yogurt
1605	Officer & A Gentleman
1606	Practices In Architecture
1607	Close The Barn Door
1608	Fish Oil
1609	Ballot Boxes
1610	Computed Tomography
1611	Little Brown Jug
1612	Open Range
1613	Quest For The Spear
1614	Green Tea
1615	White Winter Snow
1616	Mindfulness Meditation

1617	Aquaculture Methods
1618	Renewable Energy Co-Ops
1619	Hanging Guava Fruit
1620	French Toast In France
1621	Strange Relationships
1622	Sticky Notes
1623	Baby Boom Mama
1624	Empire Of The Sun
1625	Interview With God
1626	Laughing Child
1627	Fire Extinguisher
1628	Danish Pastries
1629	Last Of The Mohicans
1630	Green Spaces Utilization
1631	Pet Companionship
1632	Triangulum Galaxy
1633	Bat Cave Discovery
1634	Fish Called Wanda
1635	Pale Kings & Princes
1636	Rebel Without A Cause
1637	Video Game Graphics
1638	Stuffed Jalapenos
1639	For Richer Or Poorer
1640	Lady Sings The Blues
1641	Blackboard Rocks
1642	Organic Gardening
1643	Oddly Shaped Trees
1644	Olive Oil
1645	Egyptian Arabic
1646	Animal Rights Activism
1647	Chia Seeds
1648	Natural Skincare Routines
1649	Double Play
1650	Historical Fashion Trends
1651	The Marfa Lights
1652	Golden Summer Morning
1653	Whimsical Chirping Crickets
1654	Friedrich Nietzsche

1655	Flower Drum Song
1656	Sliding Window
1657	White Winter Scene
1658	Fielding Percentage
1659	Bizarre Banana Detective
1660	Golden Autumn Leaves
1661	Mixed Media
1662	Ghost Of Frankenstein
1663	Identity Thief
1664	Pickle Detective Mystery
1665	Iced Tea
1666	Spring Rolls
1667	History Of Language
1668	Campfires Of The Heart
1669	After The Fox
1670	Practices In Gardening
1671	Juggling Donuts
1672	Lumbar Support
1673	All In A Day's Work
1674	Hell In The Pacific
1675	Roy Rogers
1676	Flash Dance
1677	Carriage Bolt
1678	Summer Afternoon Stroll
1679	Aliens Vs. Predators
1680	Recycled Materials In Art
1681	Polar Express
1682	Gods & Generals
1683	Lucy In The Sky With Diamonds
1684	Fuller Brush Girl
1685	Jade Plant
1686	Milk Money
1687	I Believe I Can Fly
1688	Canned Tomatoes
1689	Broken Bridges
1690	Modern Period
1691	You Only Live Twice
1692	Butch Cassidy Sundance Kid

1693	Passionate Love
1694	Mastering Strategic Moves
1695	Click Here
1696	Flirting With Disaster
1697	Social Media On Society
1698	Fire Hose
1699	Love Will Conquer All
1700	Earth Girls Are Easy
1701	Fast & Furious
1702	Sour Cream
1703	The Deathly Hallows
1704	Cable Guy
1705	Army Of Shadows
1706	First Great City
1707	Tonga Bonga
1708	Expressive Writing
1709	Delhi India
1710	Cairo Egypt
1711	Bison Roaming
1712	I Love A Rainy Night
1713	Satirical Poetry
1714	Everyday Kitchen Utensils
1715	Pretzel Superhero Showdown
1716	Traditional Music Genres
1717	Relative Values
1718	Breaking Point
1719	Dinner Rolls
1720	Exploring Underwater Ecosystems
1721	I Was Born This Way
1722	Hellfighters
1723	Russian City
1724	First Contact
1725	Teen Witch
1726	Absolute Power
1727	Community Gardens Allotment
1728	Optimal Quest
1729	Fermented Vegetables
1730	Metrical Poetry

1731	Merge Sort
1732	Bells Are Ringing
1733	Traditional Storytelling Formats
1734	Stuffed Animals
1735	Apple Cider
1736	Front Page News
1737	Ghost In The Family
1738	Hyde Park On The Hudson
1739	Oat Milkhouse
1740	Rising Sun
1741	Upside Of Anger
1742	Fifth Element
1743	Construction Worker
1744	Home Alone
1745	Raiders Of The Lost Ark
1746	Lumpa Lumpa
1747	Decision Before Dawn
1748	Hex Bolt
1749	Cotton Candy Muffins
1750	Green Berets
1751	3D Printing
1752	Sunlight Requirements
1753	Magical Marshmallows
1754	Moulin Rouge
1755	The Lost City
1756	Monsters Inc
1757	Dance To The Music
1758	Early Childhood Education
1759	Relay Race
1760	Rabin-Karp Algorithm
1761	Bride Of Frankenstein
1762	Green Energy Initiatives
1763	Pigs In A Blanket
1764	Faithfull Believer
1765	Secret Ceremonies
1766	Brush Painting
1767	Creme Brulee
1768	Clinical Psychology

1769	Taming Of The Shrew
1770	Six Days Seven Nights
1771	Logical Reasoning
1772	Home Appliances
1773	Rim's Edge
1774	Whispering Leaves
1775	Cat People
1776	Sorento Hillside
1777	Bread & Tulips
1778	Stigma Reduction
1779	Spinning Pottery Wheel
1780	Green Spaces Planning
1781	Sports Drinks
1782	Illuminated Manuscripts
1783	Green Infrastructure Projects
1784	News Of The World
1785	Alphabet Blocks
1786	Nautical Mile
1787	Foxes In Mythology
1788	Underworld Evolution
1789	James Joyce
1790	Hot Summer Sun
1791	Sea Cucumbers
1792	Greatest Story Ever Told
1793	Don't Drink The Water
1794	Mochi Meme
1795	Garden Of Words
1796	Miracle Dogs
1797	Ancient Conflict Resolution
1798	Desk Set
1799	House Of Frankenstein
1800	Floyd-Warshall Algorithm
1801	Courageous Court Jester
1802	Trumpet Vine
1803	British Aerospace
1804	Big Game
1805	Butter Beans
1806	Greek Mythology Sirens

1807	Solitaire No More
1808	Santa Claus
1809	Dirty Dancing
1810	Why Me Lord
1811	Sources & Innovations
1812	Macos Monterey
1813	Eternal Flame
1814	No Mountain High Enough
1815	Clockwork Orange
1816	Incredible Hulk
1817	Enemy Below
1818	Recycled Art Projects
1819	Time Bandits
1820	Hot Chocolate
1821	Cheese Fondue
1822	Forgotten Female Inventors
1823	Coat Of Arms
1824	Quirky Glowing Fireflies
1825	Alfredo Sauce
1826	Lonely Night
1827	Wash Painting
1828	Police Officer
1829	Foot Fault
1830	Moving Talking Rocks
1831	The Extra Terrestrial
1832	Great Gatsby
1833	Pattern Tights
1834	Risky Business
1835	Terza Rima
1836	Play Tents & Tunnels
1837	Ewok Adventures
1838	Breakfast On Pluto
1839	Black Eye Galaxy
1840	Role Of Intuition
1841	Inclusive Education
1842	Edge Of The City
1843	How West Was Won
1844	Practicing Gratitude

1845	Citrus Fruit Platter
1846	Okinawan Village
1847	Natural Pet Care
1848	Frozen Lake
1849	Home Run
1850	Quantum Physics
1851	Untamed Heart
1852	Adzuki Beans
1853	Traditional Dance Forms
1854	Canis Lupus Familiaris
1855	Virgin Pina Colada
1856	Battle Of The 5 Armies
1857	Wildflower Meadow
1858	I'm King Of The World
1859	Revenge Of The Sith
1860	Oat Yogurt
1861	Life Raft
1862	Place In The Sun
1863	Green Beans
1864	Sphagnum Moss
1865	Men In Suits
1866	Fish Fillets
1867	I'll Be There
1868	An Innocent Man
1869	Don't Go Near The Water
1870	Loch Ness
1871	Planet Pirate Invasion
1872	Happy Little Child
1873	Mother's Day
1874	No Highway In The Sky
1875	Bizarre Cucumbers
1876	Santiago Chile
1877	Burn After Reading
1878	Empty Words
1879	For Greater Glory
1880	Ford Explorer
1881	Dancing Queen
1882	Thomas Crown Affair

1883	Company Of Heroes
1884	Exploring Nature's Hidden Gems
1885	Frozen Breakfast
1886	Barnyard Chickens
1887	License To Kill
1888	Voter Turnout
1889	Classical Greek Art
1890	Steamed Dumplings
1891	The Sands Of Time
1892	Cold Light Of Day
1893	Renewable Energy Fairs
1894	Absolute Beginners
1895	Simon Says
1896	Mozambican Portuguese
1897	Canned Evaporated Milk
1898	Cast Away
1899	Everyday Life
1900	New Jersey Girl
1901	Tea For Two
1902	Warm Summer Evening
1903	Sky Fell Down
1904	Gated Recurrent Units
1905	Earth Wind & Fire
1906	Vintage Vinyl Records
1907	Big Bang Theory
1908	Tofu-Based Cheeses
1909	Critic's Choice
1910	Deep Learning
1911	Fierce People
1912	Pirate Ship Adventure
1913	The Gate Of Ghosts
1914	Ice Age The Melt Down
1915	Valentine Day
1916	Avocado Butter
1917	Reliving Cinematic Magic
1918	Graphic Commander
1919	Pine Cones
1920	If I Could Turn Back Time

1921	No Vacancies
1922	Percussion Instruments
1923	Vintage Car Restoration
1924	Cosmic Academy
1925	E-Commerce Sales
1926	7 Brides For 7 Brothers
1927	Great Outdoors
1928	Bagdad Café
1929	Dog Day Afternoon
1930	Mice & Men
1931	Vanilla Sky
1932	Green Mile
1933	Blackboard Rock
1934	Science Fiction
1935	Indigenous Music Traditions
1936	Fit For A King
1937	Natural Remedies For Stress
1938	Kruskal's Algorithm
1939	Don't Break Your Promise
1940	Fellowship Of The Ring
1941	Philia Love
1942	Mustard Greens
1943	Flushed Away
1944	Promised Land
1945	AI Image Art Creation
1946	Wheel Throwing
1947	Permaculture Gardens
1948	Accidental Spy
1949	Fellowship Ring
1950	Ball Lightning
1951	Affair To Remember
1952	Tea Bags
1953	The Pianist
1954	Mister Baseball
1955	Loving You The Way I Do
1956	Talking Teapots
1957	Green Peas
1958	Companionate Love

1959	Dancing In The Street
1960	Harpsichord
1961	Microsoft Office
1962	Synchronized Swimming
1963	Dangerous Beauty
1964	Last Castle
1965	Hardwired For Action
1966	Glossy Glaze
1967	Melting Chocolate
1968	My Life In Ruins
1969	Modern Healthcare
1970	Panna Cotta
1971	Urban Wildlife Habitats
1972	Dry Chemical Extinguisher
1973	Polling Station
1974	Transportation Workshops
1975	Practical Magic
1976	Cashew Bless You
1977	Eternally Yours
1978	Bushes Wih Death
1979	Places In The Heart
1980	The Biggest Battle
1981	Hair Ties
1982	Hapax Legomenon
1983	CO2 Extinguisher
1984	French Kiss
1985	Glowing Crystals
1986	Open Heart
1987	Best Friends
1988	Cereal Bars
1989	Emergency Position
1990	Word Embeddings
1991	Speech Tagging
1992	Earning Extra Points
1993	Blossoms In The Dust
1994	Long Island Iced Tea
1995	Vikings Landing
1996	Changing Four Seasons

1997	Silence Of The Lambs
1998	Model Train Collecting
1999	Just Can't Help Believing
2000	Toy Maker
2001	Bow Ties
2002	Sinner Kissed An Angel
2003	Harlem Nights
2004	Ensemble Learning
2005	Watercolor Brushes
2006	Mysterious Glowing Butterflies
2007	Three-Legged Race
2008	Girl In The Spider's Web
2009	Aiming For The Bullseyes
2010	Love Moves In Mysterious Ways
2011	Operation Crossbow
2012	Change The World
2013	Castilian Spanish
2014	Louisiana Baton Rouge
2015	Future Innovations
2016	Public Speaking
2017	The Nature Of Man
2018	Quirky Pickle Circus
2019	Psychological Effects Of Color
2020	Only You
2021	Autoencoder Networks
2022	Pembroke Welsh Corgi
2023	Vantage Point
2024	Canned Beans
2025	Take Me Out To The Ballgame
2026	Pinch Runner
2027	Okinawan Sunrise Village
2028	Alien Glowing Crystals
2029	Tunnel Tag Football
2030	One-Eyed Jacks
2031	Fruit Juice In My Lunchbox
2032	Bridge Over Troubled Water
2033	Roman History
2034	Wondering At Celestial Beauty

2035	Medieval Art
2036	Forgotten Ancient Practices
2037	Far East Beauty
2038	Blades Of Grass
2039	Kite Runner
2040	Musical Instruments
2041	Salty Dog
2042	Ancient Whispering Statues
2043	Space Within Us
2044	Captain Courageous
2045	Zeus Let Loose
2046	Slugging Percentage
2047	English Horn
2048	Gorillas In The Mist
2049	The King & I
2050	Weather Warrior
2051	Hearts & Diamonds
2052	Saving Private Ryan
2053	Just The Ticket
2054	Roman Art
2055	All That Jazz
2056	Stewardship Of Land & Water
2057	Swagering In
2058	Comanche Moon
2059	Hardiness Zone
2060	Under Full Sail
2061	Pretty Baby
2062	Traditional Ecological Knowledge
2063	Gulf Arabic
2064	Toy Story
2065	Urban Exploration
2066	Lavender Mocktail
2067	Minimalism Lifestyle
2068	Industrial Revolution
2069	Undiscovered Country
2070	Terminator Judgement Day
2071	Lahore Pakistan
2072	Never Cry Wolf
2073	Grace Of God
2074	The Stone Angel
2075	Outdoor Learning Environments
2076	Turkish Delight
2077	Mercury Rising
2078	Blueberry Mojito Mocktail
2079	Sitting Pretty
2080	Nashville
2081	Special K
2082	Bran Flakes
2083	Knowledge In Medicine
2084	Ghost & The Chicken
2085	Open Road
2086	Pineapple Cooler
2087	Contemporary Period
2088	Three Musteteers, The
2089	Open Green Fields
2090	Wild Purple Flowers
2091	Peanut Ninja Academy
2092	Solare Eclipse
2093	Kings In The Air
2094	Pineapple Wizard Duel
2095	Ducky After All
2096	Unusual Dancing Shadows
2097	Have You Ever Loved A Woman
2098	Hera's Dragons
2099	Magnetic Resonance Imaging
2100	Frozen Smoothie Packs
2101	Friday Night Lights
2102	Sesame Street
2103	Never Burn Your Bridges
2104	Girl Happy
2105	Forbidden Kingdom
2106	Baruch Spinoza
2107	Harvey Girls
2108	I Don't Want To
2109	Lima Peru
2110	Last Samurai

2111	Greatest Showman
2112	Textile Dyeing Methods
2113	Distant Dreams
2114	North Country
2115	Potato Sack Race
2116	Garden Design
2117	Mole Operatives
2118	Unruly Flamingo Cowboy Parade
2119	Digital Camera
2120	Adopt A Highway
2121	Mysteries Of The Lines
2122	Loud Chirping Crickets
2123	Pearl Harbor
2124	Big Bounce
2125	Heart To Heart
2126	Thomas Aquinas
2127	Gouda Cheese
2128	Zany Pancake Pirate Adventure
2129	Herbal Medicine Making
2130	Open Sky
2131	Maltese Falcon
2132	Take Your Best Shot
2133	Philosophy Of Perception
2134	Son Of Kong
2135	It Started With Kiss
2136	Frozen Meat
2137	Garden State
2138	Zany Ninja Quest
2139	Radio Rebel
2140	Hundred Foot Journey
2141	Ukrainian Russian
2142	Mustard Seeds
2143	Living Challenges
2144	Mango Mocktail
2145	Enemy Of The State
2146	Solar Energy Solutions
2147	Sword Of Doom
2148	Paradise Hawaiian Style

2149	Magic Bubble
2150	Filoplume Feathers
2151	Recycled Plastic Bottles
2152	Eight Crazy Nights
2153	Knowledge Preservation Efforts
2154	Online Relationships
2155	Scent Of A Woman
2156	Ride The High Country
2157	Neapolitan Italian
2158	Digging Up Ancient Creatures
2159	Fairchild Metro
2160	Mona Lisa Smile
2161	Home Projects
2162	Jaws Under The Ocean
2163	Long Hot Summer
2164	Italian Dressing
2165	I'm Gonna Getch Yah
2166	Strangers On A Train
2167	Super Size Me
2168	Belles On Their Toes
2169	Blonde Bombshells
2170	Delay Of Game
2171	Statutory Law
2172	Aboriginal Australian
2173	Mountain Bikes
2174	Mystic Pizza
2175	Philosophy Of Art
2176	All The Things You Are
2177	Squad Goals
2178	Color Wheel
2179	American English
2180	Victory At Sea
2181	Paths Of Glory
2182	Cultural Appropriation In Fashion
2183	Groundhog Day
2184	Lotus Blossoms
2185	History Of Natural Dyes
2186	Out Of Mind

2187	Rogue Elephants
2188	Fish Sticks
2189	Display Greatness
2190	Cross Country
2191	Caramel Corn
2192	Princess Diaries
2193	Alibi Secrets
2194	Life Of Python
2195	Dump & Chase
2196	Terra Cotta
2197	Guinea Fowl
2198	Chicago Illinois
2199	Finger Painting
2200	Porsche Macan
2201	Space Camp
2202	Mushroom Heaven
2203	Rock Of Ages
2204	Seed Saving
2205	Made For Each Other
2206	Divorce Invitation
2207	Art Therapy
2208	Passed Ball
2209	Decoded Scientifically
2210	Meet The Parents
2211	Blue Hawaii
2212	Virgin Sangria
2213	Short Circuit
2214	Father Christmas
2215	Board Games
2216	Bone Broth
2217	Whole Grain
2218	Platonic Love
2219	Pest Control
2220	On Golden Pond
2221	Punt Return
2222	Red Line
2223	At Worlds End
2224	Black Windmill

2225	Our Love Affair
2226	In My Room
2227	Dictation Software
2228	The Last Crusade
2229	Hokkaido Japanese
2230	Veggie Sticks
2231	Great Race
2232	Ida! Sweet As Apple Cider
2233	Road To Bali
2234	Strategizing Moves
2235	Lenticular Clouds
2236	South Pacific
2237	A Hole In The Head
2238	Cryptocurrency Finance
2239	Dental Implant
2240	Seoul South Korea
2241	An American Affair
2242	Flashy Glowing Fireflies
2243	Vertical Gardening In Urban Spaces
2244	Shakiest Gun In The West
2245	Armageddon Is Here
2246	Naive Bayes Classifiers
2247	Every Moment Tells A Story
2248	As Young As You Feel
2249	Single Tears
2250	Science Kits
2251	Navigation Lights
2252	I Am Yours
2253	Chennai India
2254	Grey Aliens
2255	Brave One
2256	Fly Me To The Moon
2257	Moby Dick
2258	Gentlemen Prefer Blondes
2259	Pocket Full Of Miracles
2260	Break Serve
2261	Black Pearl
2262	Mississippi Jackson

2263	Life Is Like A Box Of Chocolates
2264	Man With The Gold
2265	Washington Dc United States
2266	Manchurian Candidate
2267	Always & Forever
2268	Pita Bread
2269	Five Card Stud
2270	Fire Axe
2271	Electronic Communication
2272	Potato Chips
2273	Mesmerizing Audience Illusions
2274	Advance To The Rear
2275	Effects Of Nature
2276	Arterial Gas Test
2277	Climate Resilience
2278	Across The World
2279	Urban Foraging Workshops
2280	Due Date
2281	Clock In Its Walls
2282	Bottle Shock
2283	BBQ Grilling
2284	Mini Pizzas
2285	AI In Artistic Visions
2286	Chilean Spanish
2287	Calligraphy Pen
2288	Wait Until Dark
2289	Race To Space
2290	I Haven't Time
2291	Discovering Musical Treasures
2292	Moscow On The Hudson
2293	Ballot Initiative
2294	Enemy At The Gates
2295	Theory Of Everything
2296	Opinion Polling
2297	Eagle Eye
2298	Storytelling Across Cultures
2299	Quiet Summer Morning
2300	Desperate Measures

2301	Broccoli Superhero Squad
2302	Nightely Movements
2303	How Green Was My Valley
2304	Death Defying Acts
2305	Sustainable Building Practices
2306	Return Of Serve
2307	Air I Breathe
2308	Father's Day
2309	Christmas Story
2310	Citizen Kane
2311	Bye Bye Birdie
2312	Green Transportation Initiatives
2313	Writing System
2314	Rollerball Pen
2315	Sweet Child O' Mine
2316	Five Golden Hours
2317	Symbolism In Food
2318	Mysteries Of Easter Island Statues
2319	I Want To Hold Your Hand
2320	Rough Riders
2321	Business Trip
2322	Hard Day’s Night
2323	Brie Cheese
2324	Investment Banker
2325	Finger Sandwiches
2326	Kyoto Harbor
2327	Simple Twist Of Fate
2328	Marco Polo
2329	Actions Speak Louder
2330	Defending Your Life
2331	Plant-Based Butter
2332	Three Stooges
2333	Frozen Seafood
2334	Central Intelligence
2335	Tallahassee Lassies
2336	Good Earth
2337	Squad To Squad
2338	Ballot Counting

2339	Sicilian Italian
2340	Running River
2341	Planes Trains & Automobiles
2342	For Love Or Money
2343	Human Resources
2344	Hip Replacement
2345	In The City
2346	Devil's Own
2347	Dress-Up Costumes
2348	Sense & Sensibility
2349	Wild Purple Orchid
2350	Constellation Of Orion
2351	Sorcerer's Stone
2352	Brontosaurus Landscape
2353	Guantanamo Bay
2354	Oddly Shaped Rocks
2355	Overnight Delivery
2356	All In Night's Work
2357	Traveling Merchant
2358	Sweets & Desserts
2359	Pina Colada
2360	White Wine
2361	Solar Panel Workshops
2362	Swing Shift
2363	Purple Kangaroo Circus
2364	Anchor Light
2365	Memory Game
2366	Performing Rituals
2367	Broccoli Pirate Adventure
2368	Bright Summer Day
2369	The Last Jedi
2370	Antipasto Platter
2371	Mushroom-Based Meat
2372	Long Short-Term Memory
2373	Carving Dreams Into Reality
2374	Angolan Portuguese
2375	Proud Mary
2376	Losing His Marbles

2377	Office Christmas Party
2378	Quiet Summer Evening
2379	Sugar Cookies
2380	British Bulldog
2381	Natural Language Processing
2382	African Serengeti
2383	Extraordinary Measures
2384	Golden Retriever
2385	She Wore A Yellow Ribbon
2386	Hollywood Hills
2387	Attack Ad
2388	Hyderabad Indian Lifestyle
2389	Monster In Law
2390	Guys & Dolls
2391	Pocket Door
2392	Papua New Guinean
2393	Taco Cups
2394	Table Tennis
2395	Search For Beauty
2396	Banana Nut
2397	Space Exploration
2398	Operation Pacific
2399	Teriyaki Sauce
2400	Colombian Spanish
2401	Angel Of Death
2402	Philosophy In Ethics
2403	The Money Pit
2404	Illusion Skills
2405	Mars Attacks
2406	Duck Fat
2407	Battle Of The Bulge
2408	Home Run Showdown
2409	Yorkshire Terrier
2410	Allen Wrench
2411	Water Harvesting Systems
2412	Philosophy Of Culture
2413	Cosmology & Worldviews
2414	Flight Of The Intruder

2415	Fruit Cocktail
2416	Company You Keep
2417	Fox & Hounds
2418	Ludus Love
2419	Iris Blossoms
2420	Tight Jeans
2421	Wrath Of Khan
2422	Scottish Lassies
2423	Flower Of My Secret
2424	Rolled Oats
2425	Let It Be
2426	Maryland Annapolis
2427	Significance Of Symbols
2428	New Kind Of Love
2429	Monsters Vs. Aliens
2430	Canned Anchovies
2431	Distant Thunder
2432	Greatness Waits
2433	Lemon Balm
2434	Colorful Sunset
2435	Vegan Egg Replacers
2436	Loss Functions
2437	Prehistoric Cave Art
2438	Defense Attorney
2439	Orographic Fog
2440	Counterculture Movements
2441	Whispering Wind
2442	Double Bass
2443	Living Practices
2444	Pineapple Ninja Academy
2445	African Art
2446	High Society
2447	K-Means Clustering
2448	Bending All The Rules
2449	My Love For You Is Endless
2450	Curiosity In Scientific Inquiry
2451	Bonsai Cultivation
2452	Man's Favorite Sport

2453	Rock Paper Scissors
2454	Hemp Seeds
2455	Take A Vacation
2456	Pennies From Heaven
2457	Soft Drinks
2458	Microwave Oven
2459	Pirates Of The Caribbean
2460	Precious Cargo
2461	Field Goal
2462	Palette Knife Painting
2463	Susage & Egg
2464	Looking Toward Heaven
2465	Pentagon Wars
2466	For Whom The Bell Tolls
2467	No Mercy
2468	Man In The Mirror
2469	Robin Hood
2470	Grassroots Campaign
2471	Alien Resurrection
2472	Cannellini Beans
2473	Soda Fountains
2474	Maze Runner
2475	Remote Control Toys
2476	Shakespeare In Love
2477	Bright Summer Sun
2478	Golden Summer Sun
2479	Toy Cars & Trucks
2480	Kiwi Margarita Mocktail
2481	Celery Seeds
2482	Philosophy Of Education
2483	Parties & Gatherings
2484	Cultural Diversity In Religion
2485	Banana Superhero Squad
2486	Natural Home Cleaning
2487	Hazelnut Oil
2488	Reign Of Fire
2489	Cheaper By The Dozen
2490	Empty Chair

2491	Salvation Boulevard
2492	Prostate Biopsy
2493	Lifestyle Practices
2494	Patriot's Day
2495	Silent Night Prayer
2496	Close Encounters 3rd Kind
2497	The Joshua Tree
2498	Breadth-First Search
2499	Infrastructure Implementation
2500	Voter Registration
2501	Psychology Of Conspiracy Beliefs
2502	Written Code
2503	Protecting Sensitive Skin
2504	Plumeria Blooms
2505	Miss Conception
2506	Capsule Hotel
2507	Nature-Based Education
2508	Clear Blue Water
2509	Deviled Eggs
2510	Preserving Photographic History
2511	Siberian Russian
2512	Apes Gone Wild
2513	Black Rose
2514	Semi-Supervised Learning
2515	G. I. Blues
2516	Acoustic Guitar
2517	Sombrero Galaxy
2518	Printing Press
2519	American Graffiti
2520	Yellow Lamborghini
2521	Rundown At Sundown
2522	Pizza Detective Agency
2523	Critical Condition
2524	Immanuel Kant
2525	Crashing Waves
2526	Future Scenarios
2527	Kentucky Bluegrass
2528	Felis Catus

2529	Bias-Variance Tradeoff
2530	Damsels In Distress
2531	Preserving Postal History
2532	The Final Frontier
2533	Glass Bottom Boat
2534	Witch Hunters
2535	Come & Get It
2536	Battle Angel
2537	Sunflower Oil
2538	Battle Royale
2539	Sky High
2540	He's Just Not That Into You
2541	Honest Theif
2542	Sweet Smell Of Success
2543	Basketball Hoops
2544	History Of Board Games
2545	Language Revitalization Efforts
2546	Dearly Departed
2547	Ghost Breakers
2548	Kettle Corn
2549	Internship With Philosophy
2550	The Patriot
2551	I Hear A Rhapsody
2552	Two-Point Conversion
2553	When The Swallows
2554	Pacific Rim
2555	That Old Feeling
2556	Recall Election
2557	Little Monsters
2558	Music In My Heart
2559	Lonely Heart
2560	Lord Of The Land
2561	Great Debaters
2562	Pete's Dragon
2563	Kia Sportage
2564	Western Philosophy
2565	Environmental Conservation
2566	Doberman Pinscher

2567	Give Me Shelter
2568	P.S. I Love You
2569	Sailor Of The King
2570	Fresh Morning Air
2571	Open Book
2572	Linguistic Diversity
2573	Guilt Trip
2574	Support Vector Machines
2575	Shih Tzu
2576	Renewable Energy Education
2577	Annie Oakley
2578	Babysitter's Club
2579	Endless Sky
2580	Installation Art
2581	Money From Home
2582	Apple Pie
2583	Swaying Of Trees
2584	Sustainable Agriculture
2585	Privacy In The Digital Age
2586	Pride & Prejudice
2587	Finding Neverland
2588	Inn On The Hill
2589	Canned Artichoke Hearts
2590	Geisha Boy
2591	Mesmerizing Spectators
2592	Capture The Flag
2593	Common Law
2594	Pricking Out
2595	Fruit Mousse
2596	Where's Stanley
2597	Desert Moon
2598	Rogue Nation
2599	Forgotten Ancient Civilizations
2600	Root Beer Frames
2601	Citation Mustang
2602	São Paulo Brazil
2603	Rain Man
2604	French Bulldog

2605	Transportation Solutions
2606	Gradient Boosting Machines
2607	Broken Clock
2608	Beautiful Joe
2609	Chump Change
2610	Ferns & Mosses
2611	Jumping Worms & Flying Fish
2612	Mask Of Fu Manchu
2613	On The Town
2614	Axis Of Evil
2615	Canadian Bacon
2616	Mobile Communication
2617	Concrete Poetry
2618	Food Production
2619	One Night With The King
2620	Nothing But Trouble
2621	Steam Engine
2622	Roman Holiday
2623	Good Bad & The Ugly
2624	Because I Said So
2625	Aromatic Plants
2626	VHF Radio
2627	Helen Of Troy
2628	Pagan Warrior
2629	Infinite Justice
2630	Eye Of The Beholder
2631	Ethical Wildlife Conservation
2632	Moonlight Shining Brightly
2633	Ancient Plant Medicine
2634	Rising Phoenix
2635	Crafting Letters With Elegance
2636	Decision-Making Under Pressure
2637	Traditional Agricultural Practices
2638	Orphans Of The Storm
2639	Against The Ropes
2640	Man Of The Year
2641	Home Entertainment Systems
2642	Long Long Trailer

2643	Paper Plane Contest
2644	Communication Equipment
2645	Hitchhikers Guide To The Galaxy
2646	Waist Deep
2647	Raspberry Pie
2648	Fisheries Management
2649	Malted Milk
2650	For Love Of The Game
2651	Footlight Parade
2652	Sleeping Beauty
2653	Nobody's Fool
2654	Parmesan Cheese
2655	Girls Girls Girls
2656	Youth Empowerment
2657	Warm Summer Breeze
2658	Coconut Milk
2659	Buck Privates
2660	Fixed Gear Bikes
2661	Coffee In The Morning
2662	Garden Path
2663	Ancient Artifacts
2664	Moving Rhythmically
2665	Map Of The World
2666	Indian Fighter
2667	Purple Rain
2668	Full Metal Jacket
2669	Dimensionality Reduction
2670	Half Blood Prince
2671	Eccentric Whisper
2672	Boy's Night Out
2673	Renewable Energy Storage
2674	Heal The World
2675	Fairy Godmother
2676	Natural Language Processing
2677	Waiting For The Light
2678	Direct Sow
2679	Jump Rope
2680	Chocolate-Covered Pretzels

2681	Amazing Spider-Man
2682	Moonlight Serenade
2683	Bavarian German Inn
2684	Tectonic Topography
2685	Swing State
2686	Fermented Soy Sauce
2687	Tooth Fairy
2688	Shattered Glass
2689	Cloak & Dagger
2690	Send Me No Flowers
2691	The Force Awakens
2692	Visual Communication
2693	Egg & Cheese
2694	Constant Gardener
2695	Animal House
2696	One Shot
2697	Bok Choy Garden
2698	Mistress Of The Dark
2699	Hardening Off
2700	Da Vinci Code
2701	Recumbent Bikes
2702	Endangered Species
2703	Bayside Shimmering Lights
2704	Hearts Of Darkness
2705	Stitching Tales With Threads
2706	Osaka Sunrize
2707	Adam & Eve
2708	One Flew Over The Cuckoo's Nest
2709	René Descartes
2710	Breakfast At Tiffany’s
2711	Matte Glaze Pottery
2712	Peanut Butter Conspiracy
2713	Plant-Based Yogurt
2714	Mars Needs Moms
2715	Oregano Pizza
2716	Ballad Salad
2717	For Your Eyes Only
2718	The Outsiders

2719	Rebuilding Classic Motorcycles
2720	Bermuda Triangle Unravelled
2721	Almost Famous
2722	Zany Superhero Squad
2723	Role Of Serendipity
2724	Rainwater Harvesting Systems
2725	Water Bubbler
2726	Small-Scale Farming
2727	To The Point
2728	Sparkling Water
2729	Big Fish
2730	Reading Glasses
2731	The Sound Of Music
2732	Conan The Barbarian
2733	Club Mosses
2734	Hearts Of The World
2735	Data Encryption Standard
2736	Environmental Justice
2737	Window Garden Dwellings
2738	Emergency 911
2739	Guardian Of The Gallaxy
2740	Candy Land
2741	Babe In The Woods
2742	History Of Natural Skincare
2743	Journalism & Media
2744	I Can Love You More
2745	Social Connections
2746	The Kid From Left Field
2747	Personalized Medicine
2748	Microsoft Teams
2749	Rare Plant Cultivation
2750	All The King's Men
2751	Energy & Utilities
2752	Strangers With Candy
2753	Mutual Respect
2754	Wagon East
2755	The Owl Man
2756	Born Yesterday

2757	Doughnut Detective Mystery
2758	Into The Storm
2759	Defensive Line
2760	Goat In The House
2761	Where Was I
2762	Private Resort
2763	Gotta Have Soul
2764	Jamaica Inn
2765	That Funny Feeling
2766	White Winter Landscape
2767	American Made
2768	Costume Change
2769	Tuscan Italy Village
2770	Nothing Like The Holidays
2771	Bisque-Fired Pottery
2772	Canadian Border
2773	Dances With Wolves
2774	Sweeping The Clouds Away
2775	Rare Shimmering Stars
2776	Cocoa Bean Candy
2777	Gibberish Babble
2778	Surreal Shimmering Waters
2779	Tokyo Lights
2780	Polyunsaturated Fats
2781	Roller Derby
2782	Sweet Potato Fries
2783	Paint Roller
2784	Coyote Ugly
2785	Pretzel Cowgirl Parade
2786	Reluctant Astronaut
2787	Antman & The Wasp
2788	Wandering Watermelon Mystery
2789	The Viral Factor
2790	Death In Paradise
2791	Money Monster
2792	Significance Of Tattoos
2793	Fallen Kingdom
2794	The Human Body

2795	Familial Love
2796	In Berkeley Square
2797	Blazing Saddles
2798	Raw Deal
2799	Abstract Expressionism
2800	Living Projects
2801	Enigmatic Dancing Shadows
2802	On-Base Percentage
2803	Messenger Bags
2804	Your Life Is Not Secure
2805	Remember Me
2806	Home Security Systems
2807	Yacht Club
2808	Historic Inventions & Innovations
2809	Punisher Robot
2810	Fallen Angles
2811	Elliptic Curve Cryptography
2812	City By The Sea
2813	Paint Your Wagon
2814	Once In A Lifetime
2815	Fruit Smoothies
2816	Dutch Door
2817	Cold Winter Morning
2818	Soft Green Grass
2819	Seeking Justice
2820	Inner Space
2821	Medieval Manuscripts
2822	Can't Break My Spirit
2823	Bass Guitar
2824	Addicted To Love
2825	Strange Floating Orbs
2826	Silent Whisper
2827	Fashion Expressions
2828	Pipe Wrench
2829	Take The Lead
2830	Romantic Love
2831	Transhumanism Movements
2832	Perfect Furlough, The

2833	Foreign Exchange
2834	Beneath The Crust
2835	Meet Me In St. Louis
2836	Toadstool Anthem
2837	Chronicles Of Narnia
2838	Unusual Glowing Mushrooms
2839	Jersey Devil
2840	Vampire Bat
2841	Danger Zone
2842	Teminator Salvation
2843	For Queen & Country
2844	Silent Observer
2845	More The Merrier
2846	Date With An Angel
2847	Teahouse August Moon
2848	Small Magellanic Cloud
2849	Ticking Mechanical Device
2850	High Plains Drifter
2851	His Girl Friday
2852	Eye In The Sky
2853	Keeping The Faith
2854	Snake Plant
2855	Air Force One
2856	Gucci Accessories
2857	April In Paris
2858	Digital Photography
2859	Meat & Cheese
2860	Frozen Desserts
2861	City Of Angels
2862	Haunted Mansion
2863	Center Of The World
2864	Nature Immersion Programs
2865	Basic Insticts
2866	Get Ahead In Advertising
2867	Bone Collector
2868	Over The Hill
2869	Heritage Preservation
2870	Leap Year

2871	Prelude To War
2872	Captain America
2873	Patriot Act
2874	Philosophy Of Aesthetics
2875	Most Wonderful Time Of The Year
2876	Quiet Reflections
2877	Goosebumps In The Dark
2878	Amorphous Aliens
2879	Last Action Hero
2880	Big Fluffy Clouds
2881	Magic Tricks
2882	Sesame Seeds
2883	Electric Generator
2884	London United Kingdom
2885	Shopping Blitz
2886	Pumpkin Seeds
2887	Galaxy Quest
2888	Follow That Dream
2889	Pizza Cowgirl Showdown
2890	Cosmic Expanse
2891	Karachi Pakistan
2892	Over The Rainbow
2893	Stuffed Mushrooms
2894	Five People You Meet In Heaven
2895	Paper Dolls
2896	Piper Pa-28 Cherokee
2897	Land Of The Pharohs
2898	Saturday Night Fever
2899	Extra Innings
2900	Hot Ballroom Dancers
2901	Whispering Grass
2902	Men At Work
2903	Neuroscience Of Meditation
2904	Big Country
2905	Psychedelic Art
2906	Easter Parade
2907	Almond Oil
2908	Alien Reign Of Man

2909	Romance On The High Seas
2910	Fool's Gold
2911	Return My Letters
2912	BMX Bikes
2913	The Naked Jungle
2914	An Ideal Husband
2915	Meet The Oracle
2916	The Mouse That Roared
2917	Seven Pounds
2918	Shimmering Stars
2919	Tucson Arizona
2920	The Star Chamber
2921	Rescue From Gilligan's Island
2922	Nuts & Seeds
2923	Just Like Heaven
2924	It's Only Money
2925	Never Say Never Again
2926	Thousand Island Dressing
2927	Word Processing Software
2928	Tote Bags
2929	Man I Feel Like A Woman
2930	Harpy Eagle
2931	Best Defense
2932	Human Connection
2933	Robots Recruiting Humans
2934	Animal Testing
2935	Second In Command
2936	Endless Possibilities
2937	Peach Bellini Mocktail
2938	Crab Cakes
2939	Bogotá Colombia
2940	The Runnaways
2941	Hash Browns
2942	In The Beginning
2943	Mythology Around Vampires
2944	Freedom Writers
2945	Abominable Snowman
2946	History Of Traditional Healing

2947	Don't Count Your Chickens
2948	Four Feathers
2949	Galactic Pirate Adventure
2950	Indigenous Rights
2951	Horse Gram
2952	Life Of Pi
2953	Palette Knives
2954	Mercedes-Benz Glc
2955	Sound On Emotions
2956	Long Walk Home
2957	Red River
2958	Shotgun Formation
2959	Service Line
2960	Blue Eyes
2961	Smarter Gardening Techniques
2962	Clear Blue Skies
2963	Frozen Pasta
2964	Aliens In The Attic
2965	Bringing Up Baby
2966	Shakespearean Sonnet
2967	Absentee Ballot
2968	End Game
2969	Mango Chunks
2970	Ancient Navigation
2971	Chocolate Unicorn Dream
2972	Bell Pepper
2973	Slice Of Pizza
2974	Tailwind Colors
2975	Pancake Robot Rebell
2976	Wars Never Win
2977	Pretzel Cow Showdown
2978	Dog's Purpose
2979	Community Gardening
2980	An American Werewolf In London
2981	What's Going On
2982	Cold Day In Hell
2983	Forrest Gump
2984	High Voltage

2985	Far Horizons
2986	Balancing Balls With Finesse
2987	That Touch Of Mink
2988	Mysteries Of Ancient Sites
2989	Keyboard Instruments
2990	North By Northwest
2991	Book Of Love
2992	Observing Wonders Quietly
2993	Pinwheel Galaxy
2994	Climate Change Mitigation
2995	Polka Dots & Moonbeams
2996	Dhaka Bangladesh
2997	Bacon & Egg
2998	European Vacation
2999	Rose Quartz Bouquet
3000	Air America
3001	Beggars Can't Be Choosers
3002	Bed & Breakfast
3003	Ethical Considerations In Ai
3004	From Paris With Love
3005	Occupational Therapist
3006	Second Act
3007	Surfer Dude
3008	Michigan Lansing
3009	Expert Systems
3010	Casanova's Big Night
3011	Ferry-Boat Serenade
3012	Fourth Protocol
3013	Fashion Friendly Trends
3014	The Olympians
3015	Travel & Hospitality
3016	German Countryside
3017	Easy Rider
3018	Arts & Crafts Kits
3019	Domestic Cats
3020	Catch That Kid
3021	Eight To The Bar
3022	Forgotten Ancient Languages

3023	Gnome Forests
3024	People Will Talk
3025	General Election
3026	Fostering Understanding
3027	Frozen Dumplings
3028	Radio Garden
3029	Rushing River Water
3030	Bright Sunny Weather
3031	Taco Ninja Academy
3032	Launching Miniature Marvels
3033	Hermes Powers
3034	Elephant Walk
3035	Crazy People
3036	Chicken Tenders
3037	Noah's Ark
3038	Toronto Canada
3039	Tortilla Chips
3040	Rice Pudding
3041	Belgian French
3042	Fire Blanket
3043	Service Box
3044	Green Hornet
3045	Selection Sort
3046	Computer Keyboard
3047	Galactic Disco Explosion
3048	Alpha Dog
3049	City Of The Lost Children
3050	Water Conservation
3051	Intersection Of Religion & Science
3052	Master & Commander
3053	Gone With The Wind
3054	Alabama Montgomery
3055	Soft White Sand
3056	Trade Winds
3057	California Girls
3058	Voter Id Laws
3059	Rolling Green Hills
3060	Philosophy Of Science

3061	Walnut Oil
3062	Hallways Of Chance
3063	Civic Lessons
3064	Consumption & Consumerism
3065	Model Kits
3066	Polonium Crystals
3067	Video Communication
3068	Spouting Shoots
3069	Dumpy & Lumpy
3070	Designated Hitter
3071	Old-Fashioned Apple Pie
3072	Building Intelligent Machines
3073	Fountain Pen Ink
3074	String Matching Algorithms
3075	Frozen Foods
3076	Urban Transportation Systems
3077	Barcode Scanner
3078	Summer Magic
3079	Valley Fog
3080	Harry Brown
3081	Midnight Run
3082	Girl With A Pearl Earring
3083	Peanut Butter Ninja Party
3084	Chocolate-Covered Strawberries
3085	Violation Nation
3086	Pumpkin Pie
3087	Black Panther
3088	Potato Superhero Saga
3089	Perchance Image
3090	Wonders Of Ancient Civilizations
3091	Keep The Music Playing
3092	Rococo Art & Architecture
3093	Between Strangers
3094	Operation Mad Ball
3095	First Impressions
3096	Life Jacket
3097	Austrian Highlands
3098	Great Wall

3099	Eat Pray & Love
3100	Get Out The Vote
3101	Ignorance Is Bliss
3102	Harper's Ferry
3103	Interpersonal Communication
3104	Buckaroo Bonzai
3105	End Of Watch
3106	All The President's Men
3107	Dancing Flames
3108	Green Zone
3109	The Royal Wedding
3110	Happy Gilmore - Spec Ed
3111	Caveman's Valentine
3112	Divine Secrets
3113	Circus Extravaganza
3114	History Of The Eagles
3115	Georgia Atlanta
3116	When Hell Freezes Over
3117	Quiet Winter Night
3118	Trees With Floating Orbs
3119	After Office Hours
3120	Sad Broken Hearts
3121	Human Resource Specialist
3122	Quiet Place
3123	Good Bad & Ugly
3124	Northrop Grumman Spirit
3125	Captain Corelli's Mandolin
3126	Green Building Materials
3127	Polka-Dot Elephants
3128	Whimsical Singing Frogs
3129	It Seemed Like A Good Idea
3130	Altered States
3131	Six Degrees Of Separation
3132	Pocahontas The Legend
3133	American Pie
3134	Born To Be Bad
3135	Customer Service
3136	Simply Irresistible

3137	Armed & Dangerous
3138	Small Spaces
3139	Screen Pass
3140	Symbolism In Jewelry
3141	Bicycle Repair
3142	Rice Bran Oil
3143	Cloud Atlas
3144	Stranger Than Fiction
3145	Ball Of Fire
3146	Food Sovereignty
3147	Stuck On You
3148	Quantum Computing
3149	Contributions To Society
3150	Farewell To Arms & Meet John Doe
3151	Secondhand Lions
3152	Rainbow Avalanche
3153	Tanka Toy Trucks
3154	Macarthur Park
3155	Unusual Floating Islands
3156	How To Eat Fried Worms
3157	Whistling Breeze
3158	Double Trouble
3159	Grey Owl
3160	Frozen Vegetables
3161	Strange Wilderness
3162	Memory & Collective Trauma
3163	It's A Wonderful Life
3164	Mysterious Glowing Fireflies
3165	You Can't Handle The Truth
3166	Walk Don't Run
3167	Snow Peas
3168	In The Mood
3169	Someone To Watch Over Me
3170	Rear Window
3171	Collateral Damage
3172	Red Autumn Trees
3173	Unusual Pickle Unicorn Journey
3174	Cumin Seeds

3175	Miniature Schnauzer
3176	Crafting Forms With Clay
3177	House Of Flying Daggers
3178	My Cousin Vinny
3179	Packaging Materials
3180	The Perfect Man
3181	The Power Of Ares
3182	Alternative Universe
3183	Marathon Man
3184	Drama Class Robots
3185	Charge Of The Light Brigade
3186	Blueberry Hill
3187	Walking With The Enemy
3188	Decision Making
3189	Day After Tomorrow
3190	Islands In The Stream
3191	Thirty-Nine Steps
3192	It's About Time
3193	Quill Pen
3194	Day The Earth Stood Still
3195	Taco Academy
3196	Ice Hockey
3197	Online Dating Behaviors
3198	Shoulder Bolt
3199	Swarm Intelligence
3200	Molten Metal
3201	Shining Eyes
3202	Shark Tale
3203	House Calls
3204	Cornerstone
3205	Duck Duck Goose
3206	Demystified Scientifically
3207	Pigeon Peas
3208	My Geisha
3209	Bearded Ears Sprinkle
3210	Romantic Strolls
3211	Prejudice & Bias
3212	Flight Plan

3213	Boy Toy
3214	At First Sight
3215	Night At The Museum
3216	Cargo Aircraft
3217	The Final Oracle
3218	Tickle Trees
3219	Lonely Road
3220	Soaring High Adrenaline
3221	Echoing Footsteps
3222	Big Eyes
3223	Silent Scream
3224	Ghost Busters
3225	Visual Arts
3226	For Your Information
3227	Endless Journey
3228	Digital Writing
3229	Rat Race
3230	Razor's Edge
3231	Fire Pump
3232	Argentine Spanish
3233	Download The App
3234	Canned Sardines
3235	Shade Under The Tree
3236	Legal Eagles
3237	Civil Action
3238	Stargazing In Your Eyes
3239	Wafting Floats
3240	Our Vines Have Tender Grapes
3241	Gaussian Blur
3242	Heart & Soul
3243	No God, No Master
3244	Celluloid Closet
3245	Bicentennial Man
3246	Will Of The Gods
3247	So You're The One
3248	You Can't Sit With Us
3249	Fistful Of Dollars
3250	Vegas Lights

3251	**The Last Full Measure**
3252	**Eagle & The Hawk**
3253	**Rice Porridge**
3254	**Scary Movie**
3255	**Conservation Initiatives**
3256	**Slums Of Beverly Hills**
3257	**Two Towers**
3258	**That's My Boy**
3259	**Libertine Sunrise**
3260	**Danger Is Close**
3261	**Final Analysis**
3262	**Black Swan**
3263	**Blonde & Blonder**
3264	**David Hume**
3265	**Woodwind Instruments**
3266	**Between Two Worlds**
3267	**Gummy Candies**
3268	**Night Walks**
3269	**Glass Ceilings**
3270	**Brotherly Love**
3271	**Grand Slam**
3272	**Hollandaise Sauce**
3273	**Go Tell The Spartans**
3274	**North Carolina Raleigh**
3275	**Innocents Lost**
3276	**Girl Robot Rebellion**
3277	**Judge A Book By Its Cover**
3278	**Drum Line**
3279	**Modern Times**
3280	**Pump Up The Volume**
3281	**City Lights**
3282	**Crazy Heart**
3283	**Dark Shadows**
3284	**Tall Tale Talking Trees**
3285	**Godess & Thunder**
3286	**Jenga Blocks**
3287	**Home Of The Brave**
3288	**Grapes Of Wrath**

3289	**Political Action Committee**
3290	**Deep Blue Ocean**
3291	**Tacos & Enchiladas**
3292	**Mistletoe Cactus**
3293	**Shanghai Triad**
3294	**Principal Component Analysis**
3295	**Murphy's War**
3296	**Interstellar Search**
3297	**Adventure Bikes**
3298	**Sobel Edge Detection**
3299	**The Bermuda Triangle**
3300	**One Special Night**
3301	**Electoral District**
3302	**Blast From The Past**
3303	**Urban Agriculture Practices**
3304	**Historical Myths**
3305	**Danger Diabolik**
3306	**Bitcoin Heist**
3307	**Fly Ball**
3308	**Dental Hygienist**
3309	**Chicken Wings**
3310	**Audio Communication**
3311	**Spy Games**
3312	**Dangerous Man**
3313	**Paddling Through Serene Waters**
3314	**Touring Bikes**
3315	**Fruit Tarts**
3316	**High Road To China**
3317	**Search For Eternal Love**
3318	**Uncommon Singing Frogs**
3319	**Diorama Crafting**
3320	**Over The Abyss**
3321	**Stargate Stardust Starman**
3322	**Safety Pin Dance**
3323	**Music Therapy In Mental Health**
3324	**Coconut Lime Mocktail**
3325	**Upcycling Household Items**
3326	**Raising Helen**

3327	Rights & Land Management
3328	Need For Solitude
3329	Plant-Based Alternatives
3330	The Solid Gold Caddilac
3331	Courtly Love
3332	Fun In The Sun Day
3333	Clam Chowder
3334	Painted House
3335	Rice Paddy
3336	Role Of Luck In Science
3337	I Need Somebody To Love
3338	Biohacking Biology Movements
3339	Faraway, So Close
3340	Call To Spy
3341	Sesame Oil
3342	Fire With Fire
3343	Endless Night
3344	White Christmas
3345	Velvet Beans
3346	Brazilian Jiu-Jitsu
3347	Cheeseburger Wizard Spell
3348	Playing By Heart
3349	Breakfast Sandwiches
3350	Ancient Agriculture
3351	Just Friends
3352	Neuroscience Of Learning
3353	Antique Book Restoration
3354	Wet Chemical Extinguisher
3355	Adventures Of Robin Hood
3356	Legend Keepers Shadows
3357	Draw Play
3358	The Seven Year Itch
3359	Green Living Seminars
3360	Brightest Stars In The Sky
3361	Brush Pen
3362	Pulp Fiction
3363	Black Hawk Down
3364	Don't Say A Word

3365	Ethnobotany Medicinal Plants
3366	Fire Sprinkler System
3367	Hotel For Dogs
3368	Only Angels Have Wings
3369	Wyoming Cheyenne
3370	Tomorrow Never Dies
3371	Rio De Janeiro Festival
3372	Queen's Logic
3373	BMX Racing Bikes
3374	Walk In The Woods
3375	Jack The Giant Killer
3376	Star System To Earth
3377	Corn Oil For Cars
3378	Tasmanian Devils
3379	Hot Sauce Taste Buds
3380	Cinnamon Toast Crunch
3381	Do You Care
3382	Joyful Noise
3383	New York Albany
3384	Act Of Valor
3385	Strange Historical Practices
3386	Horse Soldiers
3387	Mystic River
3388	Something Wild
3389	All Quiet On The Western Front
3390	Backhand Shot
3391	The Marrying Kind
3392	Shining Star
3393	Easy Come Easy Go
3394	Raisin Bran
3395	Weed Control
3396	Urban Green Spaces
3397	Man On The Train
3398	Cross-Country Skiing
3399	Field Of Dreams
3400	Oatmeal Cookies
3401	Hey Jude
3402	Fashion Projects For Beginners

3403	**Golden Sun**
3404	**Silver Streak**
3405	**God Must Have Sent You**
3406	**Forgotten Women Activists**
3407	**Karl Marx**
3408	**Racing Stripes**
3409	**Hidden Agenda**
3410	**Russian Siberia**
3411	**Great Expectations**
3412	**Mitsubishi Regional Jet**
3413	**Flower Nursery**
3414	**Hidden Message**
3415	**The Runaway Bride**
3416	**Cultural Diversity**
3417	**Fishing Coastal Communities**
3418	**Book Thief**
3419	**Premium Rush**
3420	**Goal Line Lunge**
3421	**Funny Farm**
3422	**Invisible Man**
3423	**Canned Foods**
3424	**Traditional Dance Performances**
3425	**Philosophy Of Mathematics**
3426	**Decoy Bride**
3427	**Action Figures**
3428	**Brute Force String Matching**
3429	**Social Worker**
3430	**Rare Handmade Shoes**
3431	**Tug Of War**
3432	**Parallax View**
3433	**Protein Smoothies**
3434	**Man From Earth**
3435	**Opal Dreams**
3436	**Modern Romance**
3437	**Tears Of The Sun**
3438	**The Winding Road**
3439	**New Hampshire Concord**
3440	**Self-Driving Cars**

3441	**Dedicated Detective Mystery**
3442	**Aircraft Carriers**
3443	**The Optimists**
3444	**Frozen Pies**
3445	**Rolling Waves**
3446	**Mobile Phone**
3447	**The Winter Soldier**
3448	**Childcare Worker**
3449	**Furry Vengeance**
3450	**Start Without Me**
3451	**Anywhere But Here**
3452	**The Skeleton Key**
3453	**Happy Go Lovely**
3454	**Hello Again**
3455	**As Good As It Gets**
3456	**Marinara Sauce**
3457	**He Ain’t Heavy**
3458	**Palm Oil**
3459	**Another Mother's Son**
3460	**Off The Chart**
3461	**Tandem Bikes**
3462	**Matchstick Men**
3463	**Tactical Gear**
3464	**Knotless Braids**
3465	**Kindness Matters**
3466	**Potting Up**
3467	**William Shakespeare**
3468	**Offensive Line**
3469	**Ancient Transportation**
3470	**Modern Philosophy**
3471	**American Renegades**
3472	**Hanky Panky**
3473	**Penalty Shot**
3474	**Mechanical Pencil**
3475	**Hot Burning Fire**
3476	**The First Avenger**
3477	**Rolling Thunder**
3478	**Steel Drum**

3479	Childhood Experiences
3480	Wildfire Firefighting
3481	Sherlock Holmes
3482	Fair Catch
3483	Father's Little Dividend
3484	Christmas Angel
3485	Hansel & Gretel
3486	Sourdough Bread
3487	Diamond Head
3488	Water Lily
3489	Ask The Dust
3490	Off The Map
3491	Garden Hose
3492	Hull Speed
3493	Beautiful Girls
3494	Burning Desire
3495	Patch Of Blue
3496	Twitching Tiger
3497	Healing Arts Therapy
3498	Early Morning Fog
3499	Behind Enemy Lines
3500	Make Believe Island
3501	Definitely Maybe
3502	Linear Regression
3503	Enchanted Dreams
3504	Cataract Surgery
3505	Communication Technology
3506	Passive Skittering
3507	Dream Girls
3508	Gradient Descent
3509	Fatty Acids
3510	Dish & The Spoon
3511	War & Peace
3512	Lonely Days
3513	Seeds Of Destruction
3514	Friends With Money
3515	Rhea Planet
3516	Track Bikes

3517	Christmas Cottage
3518	Rainbow Eucalyptus Trees
3519	Goodbye Yellow Brick Road
3520	Frozen Bread Products
3521	Mysteries Of The Manuscript
3522	Human Genetic Engineering
3523	Bits Of Jewelry
3524	Lily Of The Valley
3525	Cream Cheese
3526	Lucky Charms
3527	Welch Compression
3528	Bee Season
3529	Prince Of Thieves
3530	Dial M For Murder
3531	Recycling & Upcycling Projects
3532	Tuxedo Junction
3533	Living Networks
3534	Honeydew Melon
3535	Fountain Pen
3536	California Dreamin
3537	Cool Autumn Breeze
3538	Classic Film Appreciation
3539	International Diplomacy
3540	Robot Rebellion
3541	The Impact Of Virtual Reality
3542	Traditional Music Instruments
3543	Port Of Call New Orleans
3544	Dead Reckoning
3545	Crossfire Trail
3546	Jesus Christ Superstar
3547	Cucumber Detective Agency
3548	Street Kings
3549	Pretzel Cowboy Rodeo
3550	Remote Efforts
3551	Buffalo Soldiers
3552	Political Philosophy
3553	Land Of The Lost
3554	Fortitude Gold Rush

3555	Pirate Radio
3556	Camembert Cheese
3557	Garden Tomato Superhero
3558	Beating Broken Dreams
3559	Jaws In Space
3560	Wake My Up
3561	Kingdom's Crystal Skull
3562	Lawrence Of Arabia
3563	Arkansas Little Rock
3564	Old Fashioned
3565	Eye For An Eye
3566	Come Fly With Me
3567	Everyday Life Applications
3568	Perfect Pitch
3569	Fashion Manufacturing
3570	Raise Your Voice
3571	Cultural Homogenization
3572	Cosmic Marshmallows
3573	Unearthing Ancient Mysteries
3574	Ilyushin Il-76
3575	Foul Ball
3576	Ice Cream Mountains
3577	Rock Climbing
3578	Casualties Of War
3579	Kicking & Screaming
3580	Nature-Inspired Play
3581	Sustainable Agriculture Projects
3582	Men In Black
3583	And So It Goes
3584	Mad Money
3585	Score & Slip
3586	Unexplained Phenomena
3587	Quirky Specters
3588	Here Today Gone Tomorrow
3589	Great Dane
3590	Drums Along The Mohawk
3591	Folding Bikes
3592	Lockheed Lightning

3593	Road To Morocco
3594	Show Me The Money!
3595	Grand Canyon
3596	My Fair Lady
3597	Brandy Old Fashion
3598	Collecting Vintage Cameras
3599	Tying Flies For Fishing
3600	Traditional Dances Worldwide
3601	Renewable Energy Solutions
3602	Children Of Dune
3603	Beauty & The Beast
3604	Quark Particle Display
3605	Chicken Little
3606	Monkeys & Apes
3607	I Just Want To Celebrate
3608	Feed The Fish
3609	Bellman-Ford Algorithm
3610	Dark Of The Sun
3611	Ecosystem Restoration
3612	Time Trial Bikes
3613	Curse Of The Golden Flower
3614	Golden Compass
3615	Don't Tell The Trees
3616	Cheyenne Social Club
3617	Father Of Invention
3618	Energy-Efficient Home
3619	Unexplored Caves
3620	Don't Tell Her It's Me
3621	Milky Way Galaxy
3622	Now You See Me
3623	Laughter On Health
3624	Just Go With It
3625	From The Hip
3626	Night Of The Templar
3627	Underwater Ecosystems
3628	Folding Paper Into Art
3629	Swiss French
3630	Frozen Pizza

3631	Canned Pie Fillings
3632	Casement Window
3633	Agents On The Riverbank
3634	Minnesota In Winter
3635	Clutch Bags
3636	Who'll Buy My Bublitchki
3637	By The Light Of The Silvery Moon
3638	Liberty Stands
3639	Whimsical Talking Animals
3640	Imaginary Heros
3641	It Happened One Night
3642	Forever & Always
3643	Colby Cheese
3644	Urban Park Design
3645	The Legend Continues
3646	Car Wash
3647	Son Of Frankenstein
3648	Running Scared
3649	Bay Leaves
3650	Rule-Based Systems
3651	The Supreme Creator
3652	Freedom Rings
3653	Esoteric Traditions
3654	Kuala Lumpur Malaysia
3655	Stern Light
3656	Adjustment Bureau
3657	Asian Connection
3658	Spaceship Odyssey
3659	Bright Sunny Afternoon
3660	Whistling Wind
3661	Police Academy
3662	Sugarland Express
3663	Perfect Stranger
3664	Operation Petticoat
3665	Hot Potato
3666	Thousand Words
3667	Fire Escape Ladder
3668	Canned Salmon

3669	Dracula's Loving It
3670	Guess Who
3671	Andromeda Strain
3672	Red Light Green Light
3673	Something Of Value
3674	Finding Nemo
3675	T-Rex Battle
3676	Bringing Characters To Life
3677	May The Force Be With You
3678	Coloring Pencils
3679	Brush Pen & Ink
3680	Delta Of Venus
3681	Passion Fruit
3682	Man Of Mystery
3683	Come Back To Capistrano
3684	Sunset Boulevard
3685	One Way Passage
3686	Teenage Witch
3687	Dry Brush Technique
3688	Building His Dream House
3689	Pesky Bees
3690	Restricted Boltzmann Machines
3691	Dawn Of The Dead
3692	Three Amigos
3693	Down To Earth
3694	Running Man
3695	One Christmas
3696	Mystical Watermelon Mystery
3697	Whimsical Dancing Shadows
3698	Soybean Oil
3699	Emotional Well-Being
3700	Band Wagons
3701	Coat Of Many Colors
3702	Crafting Beer
3703	Hello Dolly
3704	Approach Shot
3705	Polling Place
3706	Psychological Effects Of Hiking

3707	Sustainable Agriculture Technology
3708	Moon Of Manakoora
3709	Wake Me When It's Over
3710	Lucky Numbers
3711	Red Summer Flowers
3712	Cheddar Cheese
3713	Candle In The Wind
3714	Operation Dumbo Drop
3715	Emerald Forest
3716	Kiss In The Dark
3717	Anger Management
3718	Speed Cruise Control
3719	Lost Empire
3720	Safe Haven
3721	Small Spiral Galaxy
3722	Lit Up A Room
3723	Labrador Retriever
3724	Biodiversity Conservation
3725	Waste Disposal Methods
3726	Silver Hawk
3727	Interior Designer
3728	Growing Mushrooms
3729	Alpha Centauri
3730	Canned Spam
3731	Ecotourism Practices
3732	Red Lentils
3733	Wrist Shot
3734	Feeling The Rhythm
3735	Dark Matter
3736	Rhythmic Gymnastics
3737	Activation Functions
3738	Option Play
3739	Placebo Effect
3740	Love Lost
3741	Monster House
3742	Urban Farming
3743	Cowboys & Aliens
3744	Role Of Empathy In Society

3745	Unmanned Aerial Vehicles
3746	Alone In The Neon Jungle
3747	Happiest Millionaire
3748	Sorry For Your Loss
3749	Free Verse
3750	Granola Bars
3751	Fear & Anxiety
3752	Fashion Designer
3753	Fruit Bat Village
3754	Port Of Call
3755	Fair Ball
3756	Rice Beans
3757	Black Dahlia
3758	Nigella Seeds
3759	Herbs & Spices
3760	Desert Rats
3761	Something Different
3762	Desert Whispering Winds
3763	Material Girls
3764	Exotic Hotel
3765	Decoration Day
3766	Pretzel Ninja Adventure
3767	Three Cornered Moon
3768	Ghost Town
3769	Indian Summer
3770	Dead Poets Society
3771	Lay Lady Lay
3772	Castaway Cowboy
3773	Alvin & The Chipmunks
3774	Broken Hearts
3775	Fishing Boats At Dawn
3776	Dwarf Galaxy
3777	Folk Instruments
3778	Superman Returns
3779	Company Of Heros
3780	Island In The Sky
3781	Cesarean Section
3782	Lonely Soul

3783	Climate Adaptation
3784	Bolt Cutter
3785	Captains Of The Clouds
3786	Social Influence
3787	Tight End
3788	Easy Come Easy Go
3789	Flaxseed Oil
3790	German Shepherd
3791	Lilac Bush
3792	Kingdom Of Heaven
3793	Salty Pretzel Superhero Squad
3794	Indigenous Food Sovereignty
3795	Legal Assistant
3796	Spice World
3797	Group Communication
3798	Summer Catch
3799	Artistic Gymnastics
3800	The World Of Tomorrow
3801	Commercial Airliners
3802	Transcendent Love
3803	Oils & Fats
3804	Bilge Pump
3805	Line Drive
3806	Raised Bed Gardening
3807	Tag Out
3808	Lose Friends & Alienate People
3809	Pound Cake
3810	Date Night
3811	Celestial Navigation
3812	History Of Traditional Medicine
3813	Artifacts Uncovered
3814	War Arrows
3815	Mystical Talking Trees
3816	Pot O' Gold
3817	If Man Answers
3818	Administrative Assistant
3819	Green Spaces
3820	Stolen Base

3821	Social Interactions
3822	Water Purification
3823	Jewel Of The Nile
3824	Bucket Sort
3825	Thicker Than Water
3826	Broccoli Cowboy Hoedown
3827	Horse Whisperer
3828	God Created Women
3829	Home Automation
3830	What Is Beauty
3831	Let's Play Cards
3832	Volunteering For Mental Health
3833	Ecstatic Vision
3834	Deepwater Horizon
3835	Embraer Family Jet
3836	Ambush Bay
3837	Vested Symbols
3838	Lion King
3839	Airbus Corporate Jet
3840	Little Trip To Heaven
3841	Gender Equality
3842	Food Security In Developing Nations
3843	Vermont In Winter
3844	Hail Ceasar
3845	Inuit Tribal Nation
3846	Raise The Main Sail
3847	Virtual Reality Technology
3848	Walking On Sunshine
3849	Positron Emission Tomography
3850	African Big Cats
3851	French Fries
3852	Drum Machine
3853	Walk The Line
3854	Ancient & Modern Influence
3855	Road Bikes
3856	Coffee Grounds
3857	Flea Flicker
3858	Boyer-Moore Algorithm

3859	**Human Relationships**
3860	**Batman Returns**
3861	**Athletic Contests**
3862	**Yolo To You Too**
3863	**Wild Pitch**
3864	**Nearness Of You**
3865	**Alternative Solutions**
3866	**Shadow Of A Doubt**
3867	**Dry Foot**
3868	**Our Home Galaxy**
3869	**Super Pac**
3870	**Fresh Summer Fields**
3871	**My Big Fat Greek Wedding**
3872	**Great Powers**
3873	**Drop Zone**
3874	**Chain Reaction**
3875	**Robinson Crusoe On Mars**
3876	**Red Supergiant**
3877	**Fruit Pies**
3878	**Morning Sunshine**
3879	**Playing For Keeps**
3880	**Cosmic Taco Invasion**
3881	**Fly Like An Eagle**
3882	**Curiosity Killed The Cat**
3883	**Concept Of Mindfulness**
3884	**Analytic Philosophy**
3885	**Generative Adversarial Networks**
3886	**There's A Girl In My Soup**
3887	**Linear Search**
3888	**Sweet Chili Sauce**
3889	**Stop-Motion Animation**
3890	**Early Modern**
3891	**Intelligence In Leadership**
3892	**Little Princess**
3893	**Return Of The Jedi**
3894	**Salwar Kameez**
3895	**Collateral Damage**
3896	**Alice In Wonderland**
3897	**Natural Home Fragrance**
3898	**Illinois Springfield**
3899	**Bay Window**
3900	**Sierra Mountains**
3901	**Rewiring The Brain's Functions**
3902	**Go Fish**
3903	**Frozen Potato Products**
3904	**Double Your Pleasure**
3905	**Down Feathers**
3906	**Toy Guitar**
3907	**Tie Clips**
3908	**Hidden Talent**
3909	**Traditional Healing Practices**
3910	**Coastal Communities**
3911	**Haiku Poetry**
3912	**Polo Shirts**
3913	**Recycled Materials**
3914	**Laughter & Mirth**
3915	**Butterscotch Pudding**
3916	**Rolling Ocean Waves**
3917	**Social Media On Mental Health**
3918	**Mozzarella Sticks**
3919	**Quick Sort**
3920	**Dirty Dozen**
3921	**Fighting Falcon**
3922	**Cheese Balls**
3923	**Patriot Games**
3924	**Index Cards**
3925	**Gung Ho**
3926	**Forbidden Planet**
3927	**Toy Tool Sets**
3928	**Automating Future Workforce**
3929	**Social Media Activism**
3930	**Ford Focus**
3931	**Sea Urchins**
3932	**Bleacher Bums**
3933	**I'll Never Smile Again**
3934	**Down With Love**

3935	Flash Of Genius
3936	Dawn Of The Planet
3937	Couples Retreat
3938	Mixed Nuts
3939	Chocolate Cake
3940	Couch Potato
3941	Say It Isn't So
3942	Caramel Apples
3943	Steel-Cut Oats
3944	It's A Mad Mad World
3945	Morning Mist
3946	Strange Chirping Crickets
3947	A Perfect World
3948	Cat In The Hat
3949	French Green Lentils
3950	Man With One Red Shoe
3951	Spray Painting
3952	Mozzarella Cheese
3953	Adventure Of Tintin
3954	Man In The Moon
3955	Astronaut Adventure
3956	None But The Loney Heart
3957	Coming To America
3958	Froot Loops
3959	An Awfully Big Adventure
3960	White Winter Frost
3961	Eye Bolt
3962	Gaucho Serenade
3963	Pennsylvania 6-5000
3964	Socket Wrench
3965	Warm Summer Day
3966	Better Than Chocolate
3967	Best Years Of Our Lives
3968	Into The Wild
3969	Villains Of The Valley
3970	Sail A Crooked Ship
3971	Recycling Programs
3972	Chicken Fat
3973	Teenage Drama Queen
3974	Glowing Trees
3975	Warm Summer Sunshine
3976	Swing Sets
3977	Energy Bars
3978	Love Can Make You Happy
3979	Flex Your Muscles
3980	Splatter Painting
3981	X-Ray Vision
3982	North Star
3983	On The Avenue
3984	Washington Olympia
3985	Mortal Thougths
3986	My Summer Of Love
3987	Marshmallow Cowboy Hoedown
3988	Automating Jobs
3989	There's No Place Like Home
3990	Stamp Collecting
3991	Princess Bride
3992	Remains Of The Day
3993	Philosophy Of Language
3994	Named Entity Recognition
3995	Road To Christmas
3996	That's Why They Call It The Blues
3997	Seeing Is Beliving
3998	Soy-Based Margarine
3999	Welcome To The Jungle
4000	Permaculture Design Workshops
4001	Black Prince
4002	Haunted Spirits
4003	Exploring Culinary Artistry
4004	Seems Like Old Times
4005	Only Forever
4006	Plant-Based Egg
4007	Solomon Islander
4008	Roquefort Cheese
4009	Lions In Africa
4010	Plant-Based Cheese

4011	**Garden Spade**
4012	**Burning Sun**
4013	**Broad Beans**
4014	**Unconditional Love**
4015	**Mumbai India**
4016	**Sorting Algorithms**
4017	**Citrus Peels**
4018	**Art & Mathematics**
4019	**Inglorious Beasts**
4020	**Bioethics Medical Dilemmas**
4021	**Here Comes-Groom**
4022	**Chattanooga Choo Choo**
4023	**Venetian Italian**
4024	**Board Games**
4025	**Mini Sandwiches**
4026	**Kidney Transplant**
4027	**Irresistible Fragrances**
4028	**Virtual Communities**
4029	**Hotel Transylvania**
4030	**Galactic Doughnut Ninja Party**
4031	**Role Of Empathy In Conflict**
4032	**Compost For Your Garden**
4033	**Give Me Liberty**
4034	**Pirates Dead Mans Chest**
4035	**Bubble Sort**
4036	**Container Gardening**
4037	**Dance Off**
4038	**Epiphytic Orchids**
4039	**Psychology Of Superstitions**
4040	**Clothing Alterations**
4041	**Atomic Bomb**
4042	**Bay Leaf**
4043	**Mysteries Of Stonehenge**
4044	**Boehemian Rhapsody**
4045	**Ancient Food Preservation**
4046	**Hidden Markov Models**
4047	**Trumpet Tribute**
4048	**Renaissance Art**
4049	**Shop Around The Corner**
4050	**One Minute To Zero**
4051	**O Brother Where Art Thou?**
4052	**Balls Of Fury**
4053	**Dark Knight Rises**
4054	**Pancake Cowboy Parade**
4055	**God Only Knows**
4056	**Men Who Stare At Goats**
4057	**Midnight Cowboy**
4058	**Dream Wife**
4059	**Caught In The Draft**
4060	**Appeal Play**
4061	**Horse With No Name**
4062	**Boer Goat**
4063	**Sophisticated Society**
4064	**Dark Morning Light**
4065	**Flight Of The Phoenix**
4066	**Unusual Shimmering Waters**
4067	**Revolutionary Road**
4068	**Show Boat**
4069	**Gray Lady Down**
4070	**Colorado Denver**
4071	**Head Of State**
4072	**Lost In Space**
4073	**Love Games**
4074	**Body Armor**
4075	**Capturing Moments**
4076	**Beijing China**
4077	**History Of Herbal Remedies**
4078	**Beautiful Mind**
4079	**Exotic Palm Trees**
4080	**Technological Singularity**
4081	**Harum Scarum**
4082	**The Skin Game**
4083	**Tea Appreciation**
4084	**Light Bulb**
4085	**Grumpy Old Men**
4086	**Legend Of The Lost**

4087	Nightingale Sang
4088	Staghorn Fern
4089	Raspberry Lemonade Mocktail
4090	Plant-Based Ice Cream
4091	Cheese & Crackers
4092	Spontaneous Human Combustion
4093	Humanitarian Intervention
4094	I Miss Your Apple Pie
4095	Public Enemies
4096	Starship Apocalypse
4097	Fatal Attraction
4098	Sixth Sense
4099	My Super Ex-Girlfriend
4100	Man Who Would Be King
4101	Fancy Pants
4102	Distant Star
4103	Stoicism Today
4104	Avengers Secret War
4105	Sunny Day
4106	Medieval Period
4107	Role Of Empathy
4108	Rascal
4109	Board Gamer Delight
4110	Mulberry Bushes
4111	Pomegranate Seeds
4112	Mom's New Boyfriend
4113	Midnight In Paris
4114	King Kong
4115	Skyscrapers Made Of Wood
4116	Blowin' In The Wind
4117	Notorious Landlady
4118	Sound Like A Broken Record
4119	Safe House
4120	Herbal Tea
4121	Utility Knife
4122	Cowboy Parade
4123	Red Summer Roses
4124	Genghis Khan

4125	Giant Spider Invasion
4126	Animal Welfare
4127	Putty Knife
4128	Wee Small Hours Of The Morning
4129	Problem Child
4130	Ballpoint Pen
4131	Recycling Programs
4132	I Dreamt I Am
4133	My Photo Vision Board
4134	On Stranger Tides
4135	Dark Knight In Daylight
4136	Crystal Oscillator
4137	Privacy Concerns Analysis
4138	Climate Change Biodiversity
4139	Lagos Nigeria
4140	Angels & Insects
4141	Moonlight & Mistleoe
4142	Happy Feet
4143	Brass Instruments
4144	The Gods Are Angry
4145	Picket Fence
4146	Piece Of Cake
4147	Better Late Than Never
4148	Attack Of The Clones
4149	Cigar Galaxy
4150	Legend Of Zorro
4151	The Passion Of The Christ
4152	Pet Detective
4153	Set The World On Fire
4154	Belly Of The Beast
4155	Pursuit Of Happiness
4156	Running Back
4157	Mindfulness In Nature
4158	Sculpting Tools
4159	Catwoman On The Prowl
4160	Dijkstra's Algorithm
4161	Beach Volleyball
4162	The New World

4163	**Double Indemnity**
4164	**The Next Level**
4165	**Fluid Identity**
4166	**Rudolph The Red Nosed Reindeer**
4167	**Running With Scissors**
4168	**Cosmic Pizza Academy**
4169	**Real Estate**
4170	**Sunny Skies**
4171	**Canned Olives**
4172	**Crimes & Misdemanors**
4173	**Ancient Healing Rituals**
4174	**Mountain Biking**
4175	**Frozen Heart**
4176	**Table For Five**
4177	**Black Tea**
4178	**Manila Philippines**
4179	**Governance Resources**
4180	**Green Lentils**
4181	**Island Of Love**
4182	**Significance Of Masks**
4183	**You Complete Me**
4184	**Hidden Treasure**
4185	**Compression Algorithms**
4186	**Chutes & Ladders**
4187	**Preservation Efforts**
4188	**Endless Love**
4189	**My Stepmother Is An Alien**
4190	**Dancing At The Blue Iguana**
4191	**Get Your Gun**
4192	**Unifying The World**
4193	**Renaissance Philosophy**
4194	**Beauty Standards**
4195	**Quiet River**
4196	**Keep Your Friends Close**
4197	**Finding Forrester**
4198	**Natural Beauty Products**
4199	**Watermelon Mint Cooler**
4200	**Cornish Hen**

4201	**Twinkling Stars**
4202	**Virginia Creeper**
4203	**Red Zone**
4204	**Hawker Beechcraft 800xp**
4205	**Early Morning Dew**
4206	**Cowgirl Ballad**
4207	**It Specialist**
4208	**Idaho Boise**
4209	**Winged Beans**
4210	**No Country For Old Men**
4211	**Symbolism In Literature**
4212	**Angel In The Family**
4213	**Swamp Fever**
4214	**Prince Of Persia**
4215	**Silver Moon**
4216	**Soy-Based Cheeses**
4217	**Climate Change Wildlifed**
4218	**Planet Of The Apes**
4219	**Artificial Intelligence**
4220	**Miater Destiny**
4221	**Cultural Identity**
4222	**Sentiment Analysis**
4223	**Goblet Of Fire**
4224	**Soil Ph**
4225	**Big Blue Sky**
4226	**Silent Movie**
4227	**Narrow Margin**
4228	**Old Mexican Town**
4229	**Party Last Night**
4230	**Diversity In Storytelling**
4231	**Natural Cleaning Products**
4232	**Pass Interference**
4233	**Crafting Words Meticulously**
4234	**Prairie Home Companion**
4235	**Armored Vehicles**
4236	**Just The Way You Are**
4237	**Social Media On Communication**
4238	**Starting Out In The Evening**

4239	On The Beach
4240	Porsche Cayenne
4241	One In The Chamber
4242	Balance & Checks
4243	Convolutional Neural Networks
4244	Nut-Based Cheeses
4245	Brick Mansions
4246	Skull Island
4247	Automotive Industry
4248	Into The West
4249	Social Media On Culture
4250	Good Vibrations
4251	Moonrise Kingdom
4252	Draft Day
4253	The Time Machine
4254	Lake House View
4255	The Prince & Me
4256	Plant-Based Milk
4257	Boeing Stratofortress
4258	Indoor Gardening
4259	Sea Urchin
4260	All I Want For Christmas
4261	Train Sets
4262	Nut Butters
4263	Soul Mate Sketch
4264	Government Mint
4265	Bundt Cake Heaven
4266	Live & Let Live
4267	Activists & Their Impact
4268	Hole In The World
4269	Dramatic Pickoff
4270	Laws Of Attractions
4271	Provolone Cheese
4272	Mini Meat Pies
4273	Relief Pitcher
4274	Mai Tai
4275	The High Priests
4276	Classical Period

4277	One Last Dance
4278	Inside Job
4279	George Of The Jungle
4280	Rights & Self-Determination
4281	On Deadly Ground
4282	Hologram For The King
4283	Great Pyramids
4284	Large Magellanic Cloud
4285	Pineapple Chunks
4286	Bells Of St Mary
4287	Corned Beef
4288	Prisoner Of Second Avenue
4289	Boo-Hoo Delusions
4290	Soul Surfer
4291	Seven Samurai
4292	Plant-Based Meat
4293	Deer Hunter
4294	Sports Equipment
4295	Jingle All The Way
4296	Laparoscopic Surgery
4297	Coupling Nut
4298	A Walk To Remember
4299	Vast Technology
4300	Snakes & Ladders
4301	Pumpkin Seed Oil
4302	Body Image
4303	Red Wine
4304	Some Like It Hotu
4305	Puss N Boots
4306	House In Umbria
4307	Ancient Storytelling
4308	An American In Paris
4309	Aquaman In The Lagoon
4310	Transformer Models
4311	Social Media Influencers
4312	Standing Stones
4313	Crime Of The Century
4314	Napoleaon Dynamite

4315	Ocean's Twelve
4316	Universal Love
4317	Hero At Large
4318	Magical Unicorn Journey
4319	Inspector's Mysteries
4320	Stencil Painting
4321	Cultural Diversity In Art
4322	Double Identity
4323	Feature Engineering
4324	Seven Little Foys
4325	Make My Day
4326	History Of Natural Remedies
4327	Prince Of Foxes
4328	Cutthroat Island
4329	Lost Hope
4330	Swing Vote
4331	Glaze Brush
4332	Mature Love
4333	Elegant Stone House
4334	Naive Bayes Classifier
4335	Cheese Doodles
4336	Room For One More
4337	Golden Summer Sunset
4338	Bunny Rabbits
4339	Cleopatra's Palace
4340	Permaculture Design Courses
4341	Griping Landscape
4342	Prevent Defense
4343	Out Of Reach
4344	Lost Soul
4345	Follow Me Boys
4346	Creativity Levels
4347	Layer Cake
4348	Dark Money
4349	Night & Day
4350	Breakfast Bars
4351	Modigliani
4352	Fermented Fish Sauce

4353	Dwelt In Harlem
4354	Girl Who Played With Fire
4355	Scorpion King
4356	Mirror Masks
4357	Bermuda Grass
4358	Virginia Woolf
4359	Playing Gin
4360	Psychological Effects
4361	Sudden Impact
4362	Maple Syrup Pancakes
4363	Tennessee Nashville
4364	Risk-Taking Behavior
4365	Pot Of Gold
4366	Ballot Measure
4367	British English
4368	Adbduction
4369	Campaign Trail
4370	Divine Union
4371	Cheese Sticks
4372	Sixteen Candles
4373	Million Dollar Arm
4374	Mint Julep
4375	Busted Chain
4376	Healing Power Of Music
4377	Toy Blasters
4378	Coincidence In History
4379	Four Weddings & A Funeral
4380	Moscow Russia
4381	Godzilla Vs. Kong
4382	Riding Waves
4383	Prickly Pear Desert
4384	Keffiyeh Patterns
4385	A Cold Winter's Night
4386	Another Stakeout
4387	It Happens Every Spring
4388	Farmer's Daughter
4389	Machine Learning
4390	Maidenhair Fern

4391	Performance Art
4392	Guinea Pigs
4393	Quiet Summer Night
4394	Ethical Investing
4395	Poll Watcher
4396	Green Book
4397	Stand-Up Comedy
4398	Lost City Of Atlantis
4399	Oh, God! Book Ii
4400	Purple Haze
4401	Something Borrowed
4402	Cool Summer Breeze
4403	Worcestershire Sauce
4404	Absence Make Hearts Stronger
4405	Inconvenient Truth
4406	Come Blow Your Horn
4407	Meat & Poultry
4408	Uncommon Dancing Flames
4409	Sword Beans
4410	Men In Thights
4411	Silk Stockings
4412	Native Plant Gardening
4413	Cyclocross Bikes
4414	Forbidden Subjects
4415	Face-To-Face Communication
4416	Country Strong
4417	One Fine Day
4418	Casablanca Express
4419	Captain Marvel
4420	Fire Hydrant
4421	To The Ends Of Earth…
4422	Ghost In The Shell
4423	Young Doctor's Notebook
4424	Road Cycling
4425	Methods Of Food Preservation
4426	Pry Bar
4427	Black Beans
4428	Pop Art

4429	Bizarre Chirping Birds
4430	Million Dollar Baby
4431	Astronaut Farmer
4432	Kindergarten Teacher
4433	Political Party
4434	Anchor Bolt
4435	Ancient Egyptian Pyramids
4436	Manna From Heaven
4437	Waste Reduction
4438	Sukhoi Superjet 100
4439	History Of Traditional Crafts
4440	Contemporary Philosophy
4441	Raku Kiln Pottery
4442	Christmas Clause
4443	Starting Over
4444	Chickpea-Based Meat
4445	Building Miniature Worlds
4446	Toy Animals & Figures
4447	Flax Milk
4448	Powdered Milk
4449	Fyodor Dostoevsky
4450	Depth-First Search
4451	Green Spring Grass
4452	Cycling Infrastructure
4453	Little Fish
4454	Another Thin Man
4455	Summer Rental
4456	Stitching Memories Into Fabrics
4457	Social Media On Self-Esteem
4458	We Were Stangers
4459	Adobe Illustrator
4460	Blue Sky
4461	Ice Fog
4462	Into The Blue
4463	My Darling Clementine
4464	Front Of The Line
4465	Wing & A Prayer
4466	Edible Garden Projects

4467	Gallipoli
4468	Potter's Wheel
4469	Greek Yogurt
4470	Fashion Design Projects
4471	Knuth-Morris-Pratt Algorithm
4472	Cargo Bikes
4473	Random Forests
4474	Focus On Love
4475	Cavalier Spaniel
4476	Edge Of Darkness
4477	Clan Of The Cave Bears
4478	Inside Man
4479	Mozart & The Whales
4480	Building Blocks
4481	Storge Love
4482	Grape Juice
4483	Metropolis Rising
4484	Candy Man
4485	March Of The Penguins
4486	Watermelon Cowboy Ballad
4487	Before Sunset
4488	Computer Vision
4489	The Metonic Cycle
4490	Pistachio Oil
4491	Chinese Checkers
4492	Ladies In Lavender
4493	Any Wednesday
4494	Frozen Entrees
4495	Rings The Bell
4496	Andromeda Galaxy
4497	Enter The Dragon
4498	Texas Austin
4499	Manhattan Mystery
4500	Lupini Beans
4501	Artificial Heart
4502	Spoken Word Poetry
4503	A House Is Not A Home
4504	Eastern Philosophy

4505	Water Hyacinth
4506	Mental Well-Being
4507	Stealth Talking Animals
4508	American President
4509	Muses Hercules
4510	Harry Potter &
4511	Social Equity
4512	Wee Bit O' Revolution
4513	Ancient Construction
4514	I'd Know You Anywhere
4515	Body Of Lies
4516	Medieval Philosophy
4517	Darling Companion
4518	Milkshake Heaven
4519	Ghosting The Future
4520	Transfer Learning
4521	Ancient Egyptian Art
4522	Fiddler Crabs
4523	Mystical Talking Animals
4524	Collecting Rare Coins
4525	Double Fault
4526	Space Odyssey
4527	Steel Magnolias
4528	Angels Over Broadway
4529	Savage Heart
4530	Fashion Trends
4531	Every Cloud's Silver Lining
4532	Rolling Stones
4533	The Nazca Lines
4534	Healing Practices & Wellness
4535	Sparkling Apple Cider Mocktail
4536	Lady & The Tramp
4537	Early Voting
4538	Night Passage
4539	Social Capital
4540	Tall Majestic Trees
4541	Voter Fraud
4542	Conquest Of The Apes

4543	Uncanny Glowing Fireflies
4544	Fallen Leaves
4545	Flight Feathers
4546	European Portuguese
4547	Upcycling & Repurposing
4548	End Zone
4549	Down The Line
4550	Wandering Wizard Spell
4551	Bring It On Again
4552	Rare Birds Of Prey
4553	Legally Blonde
4554	Independence Day
4555	Ball Toss
4556	Man Of The House
4557	Invasion Of Aliens
4558	Crazy Eights
4559	Utah Salt Lake City
4560	Neural Networks
4561	Moscow Mule
4562	Primary Election
4563	Chess Competition
4564	Toast Slowdown
4565	Cosmic Cowboy Ballad
4566	Coriander Seeds
4567	Shrimp Cocktail
4568	Long Cool Woman In A Black Dress
4569	Beautiful Country
4570	Ant Bully
4571	Gridiron Gang
4572	Forever & Ever
4573	Ocean’s Eleven
4574	Vegetable Oil
4575	Ice Cream
4576	Broken Trail
4577	Whimsical Purple Unicorn
4578	Tape Measure
4579	Wire Cutters
4580	Nine To Five

4581	Air Conditioning
4582	New Arrangement
4583	Urban Farming Initiatives
4584	Achilles Heel
4585	Green Trees
4586	Mung Beans
4587	Martial Arts Training
4588	Direct Examination
4589	Film Festivals
4590	Vivid Hallucination
4591	Point Of No Return
4592	Boston Fern
4593	Do No Harm
4594	Checking Line
4595	Birds Of Paradise
4596	The Shaggy Dog
4597	Passing Shot
4598	Foam Extinguisher
4599	Women's Rights Movements
4600	Uncanny Whispering Winds
4601	Warm Summer Sun
4602	School Of Rock
4603	Zebra Plant
4604	Runs Batted In
4605	To Seize & Hold
4606	Unconventional Shimmering Stars
4607	Cold Winter Day
4608	Final Countdown
4609	Military Personnel
4610	Correction Tape
4611	Broken Arrow
4612	A Knight's Tale
4613	Sea Of Trees
4614	Major League
4615	Feta Cheese
4616	Avocado Oil
4617	Reviving Classics
4618	Hercule's Power

4619	**Bombardier Global Express**
4620	**Black & White**
4621	**Anise Seeds**
4622	**Talking Rocks**
4623	**Natural Building Techniques**
4624	**Adam's Rib**
4625	**Battteries Not Included**
4626	**Rise Of The Machines**
4627	**Birds Of Prey**
4628	**Baby Yeti Sasquatch**
4629	**Dancing Trees**
4630	**Deep Blue Sea**
4631	**Hair Clips**
4632	**Shetland Sheepdog**
4633	**That's The Way Of The World**
4634	**Bless The Beast & Children**
4635	**Rubber Duckie You're The One**
4636	**Terminal Velocity**
4637	**Deal Of The Century**
4638	**Coconut-Based Cheeses**
4639	**Soy Yogurt**
4640	**Spading Mother Earth**
4641	**Rugby Action**
4642	**Mcdonnell Douglas**
4643	**Post Hole Digger**
4644	**Prickly Pear**
4645	**Best Men**
4646	**Shattered Hopes**
4647	**Nighttime Photography**
4648	**Voyage At The Bottom Of The Sea**
4649	**Just For You**
4650	**Standard German**
4651	**Histogram Equalization**
4652	**Non-Verbal Communication**
4653	**Accidental Husband**
4654	**Ho Chi Minh City Vietnam**
4655	**Reindeer Games**
4656	**My Favorite Martian**

4657	**Real Genius**
4658	**Rights & Sovereignty Movements**
4659	**Peanut Butter Cowboy Hoedown**
4660	**The Dark World**
4661	**High On A Windy Hill**
4662	**Philosophy Of History**
4663	**Speed Racer**
4664	**Fools Rush In**
4665	**Rice Milk**
4666	**Holiday To Remember**
4667	**I'm Nobody's Baby**
4668	**Nutty Professor**
4669	**Courtship Of Eddie's Father**
4670	**Binary Search**
4671	**Capturing Celestial Beauty**
4672	**Lonely Teardrops**
4673	**Bend In The River**
4674	**Ebony & Ivory**
4675	**Hidden Path**
4676	**General Dynamics**
4677	**Prim's Algorithm**
4678	**Life Ring**
4679	**Uncanny Shimmering**
4680	**Clamp Down**
4681	**Above The Law**
4682	**Cinnamon Basil**
4683	**City Bikes**
4684	**Beauty School Dropout**
4685	**Quirky Singing Birds**
4686	**Jack & Jill Adventures**
4687	**Digital Privacy Laws & Ethics**
4688	**Thin Ice**
4689	**Urban Food Forest Projects**
4690	**Conspiracy Theory**
4691	**Disorganized Crime**
4692	**Energy Solutions For Homes**
4693	**Dogs & Cats**
4694	**Heaven Can Wait**

4695	Gaming & Entertainment
4696	Audio Sound Check
4697	Deck The Halls
4698	Square Nut
4699	Blank Verse
4700	Never An Old Maid
4701	Wisconsin Madison
4702	Frozen Burritos
4703	Truck Driver
4704	Journey To The Center Of Earth
4705	Digital Divide
4706	Upcycled Home Decor
4707	Natural Cosmetics
4708	Chariot Racing
4709	Mania Love
4710	Wandering Cowboy Circus
4711	Verbal Communication
4712	Environmental Philosophy
4713	At The End Of The World
4714	Devil's Brigade
4715	Loud Singing Frogs
4716	Connecticut Hartford
4717	Textured Vegetable Protein
4718	Home Energy Solutions
4719	Hough Transform
4720	Listen To The Music
4721	Surf's Up
4722	Rustling Leaves
4723	Grass Harp
4724	Levantine Arabic
4725	Watermelon Seeds
4726	My Way
4727	Empty Heart
4728	Mercedes-Benz E-Class
4729	Singin' In The Rain
4730	Lion In The Desert
4731	Catch & Release
4732	Beyond Borders

4733	Haunted Honeymoon
4734	Freeze Tag
4735	Counting Is Fun
4736	Monterey Jack Cheese
4737	Minority Report
4738	Ancient Healing Traditions
4739	Potential Of Psychedelics
4740	Into The Sun
4741	Human Rights In The Digital Age
4742	Rare Singing Frogs
4743	Handmade Broken Arrow
4744	Kansas Topeka
4745	Pink Panther Strikes Again
4746	Back To Bataan
4747	Philosophy Of Religion
4748	Mark Of The Vampire
4749	Life As We Know It
4750	Double Wedding
4751	Digital Nomadism
4752	I'd Rather Be Rich
4753	Exit Poll
4754	National Treasures
4755	You've Got Me This Way
4756	Beechcraft Bonanza
4757	Beat The Devil
4758	Acorn Nut
4759	Home Renovation Projects
4760	Contempt Of Court
4761	Murphy's Law
4762	No Man Is An Island
4763	Nevada Carson City
4764	Artistic Graffiti
4765	Our Nearest Star
4766	Siberian Husky
4767	Fermented Tofu Fuyu
4768	Deep Blue Sky
4769	Romancing The Stone
4770	Shattered Dreams

4771	Brown Bats Circling
4772	Back To The Future
4773	Wine Corks
4774	Do Not Disturb
4775	Shaping Miniature Trees
4776	Butterfly Effect
4777	Lager Festival
4778	Wizard Spell
4779	Slab Building
4780	Egg & Spoon Race
4781	Whirling Dervish
4782	Tall Green Trees
4783	Benefit Of The Doubt
4784	Angels In America
4785	Fashion Events
4786	Bright Orange Sun
4787	Negative Campaigning
4788	Forest Bathing
4789	Not Guilty
4790	Science Of Dreams
4791	King Arthur
4792	Sound Of Music
4793	Fairy Tale Story
4794	Recycled Materials In Crafts
4795	Contemporary Art
4796	Military Aircraft
4797	Curse Of The Judea Chalice
4798	Batman Forever
4799	Fast Runner
4800	The Mummy
4801	Discovering Hidden Treasures
4802	Slotted Nut
4803	Philosophy Of Psychology
4804	Classical Music Composers
4805	Back To School
4806	Green Smoothies
4807	Frozen Appetizers
4808	Dead Men Don't Wear Plaid

4809	Spirit Of St. Louis
4810	Rice Krispies
4811	Mini Burgers Sliders
4812	Drop Dead Gorgeous
4813	Ground-Rule Double
4814	Sumo Wrestlers
4815	Fat Cattle
4816	Whimsical Pizza Wizard Duel
4817	Instructions For Visions
4818	Niagra Falls
4819	Chance In Evolution
4820	Quebec French
4821	Shenzhen China
4822	Father Of The Bride
4823	Key Largo
4824	Gentleman's Agreement
4825	Five O'clock Whistle
4826	Please Don't Eat The Daisies
4827	Cochlear Implant
4828	A Different Corner
4829	Non-Profit Organizations
4830	Philosophic Knowledge
4831	Asphalt Jungle
4832	Sushi Dragon Parade
4833	Silent Night
4834	Orange Juice
4835	Darn That Dream
4836	Charlie & The Chocolate Factory
4837	Silver Linings
4838	Moroccan Arabic
4839	Ants In The Pants
4840	Extraordinary Gentlemen
4841	Social Media Addiction
4842	Toy Trains
4843	Cosmic Adventurer
4844	Graceful Shimmering Waters
4845	Closest Known Star
4846	Desktop Computer

4847	Affectionate Love
4848	Breezey & Me
4849	Man-To-Man Coverage
4850	Great Women Pioneers
4851	Whirlpool Galaxy
4852	Shanghai Knights
4853	Strange Laws Around The World
4854	Ways Of The West
4855	Lost In Your Eyes
4856	Streetlights Illuminating Moods
4857	Tumbling Moonlight Tango
4858	Chickpea Flour
4859	Short Track Speed Skating
4860	Could It Be Magic
4861	Home Improvement Projects
4862	Internal Combustion Engine
4863	Another You
4864	Dangling Participles
4865	Tell No One
4866	Let Sleeping Dogs Lie
4867	Urban Greenmanagement
4868	Stress Reduction Programs
4869	It Should Happen To You
4870	Smoke Detector
4871	Traditional Storytelling Methods
4872	Home Decor Projects For Families
4873	Molding Forms With Hands
4874	Cultural Appropriation In The Arts
4875	Something's Got To Give
4876	Cocoa Butter
4877	The Art Of War
4878	Earned Run Average
4879	Hilly Grasslands
4880	Here's Johnny
4881	Suburban Girl
4882	Companion Planting
4883	International Intrique
4884	Icing On The Cake

4885	Biohacking Citizen Science
4886	Bizarre Rock Formations
4887	Doll Clothing
4888	Whimsical Glowing Fireflies
4889	Jet Pilot
4890	Collateral Beauty
4891	One Way Out
4892	Habits Of Earthbound Human
4893	You've Got Mail
4894	Fantastic Beasts
4895	The Other Conquest
4896	The Trance
4897	Homeland Security
4898	Unusual Talking Trees
4899	Alternative Models
4900	My Girlfriend's Boyfriend
4901	Prize Winner
4902	Rooftop Gardening In Urban Areas
4903	Philosophy Of Altruism
4904	Deep Belief Networks
4905	Marketing & Advertising
4906	Pool Float
4907	Dark Night
4908	Mask Of Zorro
4909	Philosophy Of Mind
4910	Nothing But The Truth
4911	Heaven Is For Real
4912	Pan's Labyrinth
4913	Adjustable Wrench
4914	Effects Of Gardening
4915	Søren Kierkegaard
4916	Shall We Dance
4917	Electric Keyboard
4918	Event Planner
4919	Medusa’s Fortnite
4920	When Nature Calls
4921	Logistic Regression Models
4922	Executive Decision

4923	**Mountain Bikes**
4924	**The Saint**
4925	**Demolition Man**
4926	**Hot Dancing Flames**
4927	**Bishop's Wife**
4928	**Philosophy Of Law**
4929	**Concerts & Performances**
4930	**Monkey Business**
4931	**Final Cut Pro**
4932	**Chicken Noodle**
4933	**Water Lettuce**
4934	**Blackboard Jungle**
4935	**Bow Window**
4936	**Dairy Products**
4937	**Show Me The Money**
4938	**Snow White & The 7 Dwarfs**
4939	**Duel In The Sun**
4940	**Ancient Mayan Civilization**
4941	**Hidden Meaning**
4942	**Summer Place**
4943	**Liver & Onions**
4944	**Split Peas**
4945	**You Are My Sunshine**
4946	**Written Communication**
4947	**The Sea Is Watching**
4948	**Missouri Jefferson City**
4949	**Feeding The World**
4950	**Smith Goes To Washington**
4951	**Where Do We Go From Here**
4952	**Quail Eggs**
4953	**The Smallest Show On Earth**
4954	**It's A Blue World**
4955	**City Of Ghosts**
4956	**Charles Dickens**
4957	**I Don't Give A Hoot**
4958	**Ice Harvest**
4959	**Ghosthunter Search**
4960	**Absolute Deception**

4961	**Montana Helena**
4962	**Spider-Man**
4963	**Gps Navigation System**
4964	**Peanut Brittle**
4965	**Quantum Mechanics**
4966	**Swiss Chard**
4967	**Observing Celestial Wonders**
4968	**Distant Memory**
4969	**Pancho Villa**
4970	**Solved Scientifically**
4971	**Whimsical Talking Trees**
4972	**Digital Piano**
4973	**Johnny B Goode**
4974	**Tethered Floating Cities**
4975	**Hemp Milk**
4976	**Galindez File**
4977	**Toy Piano**
4978	**Play Kitchen Sets**
4979	**Pinch Hitter**
4980	**Hasta La Vista Baby**
4981	**Soy Milk**
4982	**Her Alibi**
4983	**Hit By Pitch**
4984	**Rocks Of The High Hills**
4985	**Proxima Centauri**
4986	**Paris France**
4987	**Hell To Eternity**
4988	**Time Travel**
4989	**From Here To Eternity**
4990	**Solar Projects**
4991	**Education & Curriculum**
4992	**Fireflies In The Garden**
4993	**Black Book**
4994	**Cranberry Beans**
4995	**High Floating Islands**
4996	**Secrets Waiting To Be Discovered**
4997	**Bucket List**
4998	**Rolling Clouds**

4999	Eye Of The Tiger

5000	Riding To The Moon

By now, you've learned how to create your own amazing list of creative prompts. Continue testing your favorite prompts with different models and styles.

HERE ARE SOME SILLY PHRASES YOU MAY ALSO WANT TO TEST

You've Got A Hungry Friend
Happy Birthday
Graduated From High School
Sorry You Lost
You Remembered
Thinking Of You
You've Learned To Swim
Thank You
Sorry I Missed Our Date
Please Forgive
Happy Anniversary
I'm Really Sorry
First Day Of Summer
For The Paper Boy
Welcome Back
To Help Your Forget
To Your New Job
For Your Hair Stylist
Graduation From College
Happy Mother's Day
Great Show
For The Gardener
First Grade Graduation
For My Minister
Offering A Sweet Bribe
Job Promotion
Washing My Car
Happy Father's Day
For My Pets
Happy Valentine's Day
New Hair Colors
Plastic Surgery Success
Pick A Hot Stock

Thanks For Being You
For The Maid
Hello From England
Accepted Into Medical School
You've Learned To Drive
Fixing My Flat Tire
I Like You
It Was A Lot Of Fun
The Season Is Over
I Quit Smoking
Happy Hanukkah
For A Stocking Stuffer
Thanks For A Back Rub
For My Babysitter
You've Having A Baby
Thanks For Doing The Dishes
My Personal Trainer
Farwell Dear Friend
Thanks For A Great Dinner
Your 1st Day In High School
I Love You
You've Learned To Dance
Accepted Into College
Remember Me
For The Car Porter
New Love
Housewarming Party
Mowing The Lawn
Our New House
Your 1st Day In College
Merry Christmas
Don't Marry A Millionaire
You Married A Millionaire

First Day Of Sprint
Here's Candy & Flowers
Grooming Our Dog
Opening A New Business
You Look Great
First Day Of Winter
Sorry I Missed Your Birthday
For My Work Out Partner
Our New Apartment
For My Rabbi
Get Over That Cold Soon
I Lost Ten Pounds
I Quit Drinking
1st Day In Kindergarten
I Want You To Like Me
We're Getting Divorced
For No Reason At All
Sorry The Market Dropped
Don't Retire Refocus
Shoveling The Walkway
Get Well Soon
You Played Great
You Got A New Pet
Accepted Into Law School
Please Write
You're Joining The Military
Please Write
Can I Use Your Car
Welcome Home
Happy New Year
It's A Great Party
Thenks For The Haircut
Please Call Me
First Day Of Fall

HERE'S SOME SINGLE WORD PROMPTS YOU MAY ALSO WANT TO TEST

Abalone	Alley	Arcane	Avuncular	Beagle
Abayas	Allspice	Archery	Aymara	Beanies
Abjure	Almonds	Architect	Azalea	Bears
Abrogate	Aloe Vera	Architecture	Backcheck	Beautiful
Abscond	Altima	Arcturus	Backer	Beavers
Abstract	Aluminum	Ardent	Background	Beef Fat
Abstraction	Amalgamate	Aristotle	Backhand	Beekeepers
Abstruse	Amaranth	Arrange	Backpacks	Beetles
Academic	Ambassador	Arrogant	Badger	Beetroot
Accent	Ameliorate	Artemis	Badminton	Begin
Accept	Amhara	Artichoke	Bagels	Beginner
Accomplisher	Amorphous	Artifice	Bagpipes	Belgian
Accord	Amused	Artisans	Baklava	Believe
Accordion	Anacharis	Artist	Balalaika	Believers
Acerbic	Anathema	Artistic	Balance	Bellicose
Achieve	Anchor	Arugula	Balatron	Belts
Achiever	Anchovies	Ashanti	Ball Bearing	Benefit
Ackee	Ancient	Askance	Ball Toss	Bengali
Acorn Nut	Ancillary	Asparagus	Ballad	Berber
Acquiesce	Andouille	Asperity	Balloons	Berries
Acrostic	Angular	Assail	Ballot	Beverages
Action Painting	Animals	Assault	Balsamic	Biathlon
Activator	Animated	Assessor	Bamboo	Bibelot
Actuality	Animus	Assiduous	Banana	Bicycle
Address	Anklets	Assist	Banana Nut	Biennial
Administrator	Annihilate	Astronomy	Banausic	Big
Admire	Annual	Aswang	Bandanas	Bigfoot
Adroit	Anodyne	Athena	Bangles	Bike
Advance	Answer	Athletics	Banjo	Bilious
Advantage	Antares	Atlas	Banshee	Binder
Advisor	Anteaters	Atmospheric	Baritone	Biofuels
Advocate	Apache	Atropos	Barley	Biography
Aesthetic	Aphrodite	Attack Ad	Barn Door	Biomorphic
Affidavit	Apocryphal	Attainer	Barnacles	Birch
Afrikaner	Apollo	Attenuate	Baroque	Birds
Agile	Apostasy	Attorney	Base Hit	Biscotti
Aglet	Apothegm	Attractive	Baseball	Bisque
Agreement	Appeal	Audacious	Baseline	Black & White
Airbus	Appear	Audible	Basil	Black Tea
Aircraft	Apple Pie	Augury	Basilisk	Blackberry
Airplane	Appraiser	Authentic	Basket	Bland
Akimbo	Appropriation	Author	Bass Drum	Blatant
Alacrity	Apricot	Automatism	Bassoon	Blazers
Albatross	Arabic	Avant-Garde	Batik	Blithe
Alchemy	Arachnids	Avatar	Battery	Blitz
Aleatory	Arbiter	Avengers	Bauhaus	Blizzard
Aliens	Arbitrator	Avocado	Bay Leaf	Blouses
Allay	Arbors	Avoid	Bbq Sauce	Bloviate

- Bludgeon
- Blue Eyes
- Blue Line
- Blue Sky
- Blueberry
- Bmx Bikes
- Boarding
- Bobsleigh
- Bok Choy
- Bologna
- Bombastic
- Bone Broth
- Boombox
- Boots
- Bouzouki
- Bow Light
- Bow Ties
- Bowline
- Bowties
- Boxers
- Boxing
- Boxster
- Boxwood
- Bracelets
- Brash
- Bratwurst
- Brave
- Break
- Breakaway
- Briefcase
- Bright
- Brocade
- Broccoli
- Brown Bat
- Brownies
- Brush Pen
- Brushes
- Brushwork
- Buckwheat
- Bucolic
- Build
- Builder
- Buildings
- Built
- Bulgur
- Bulldog
- Bullpen
- Burnish
- Bushes
- Busy

- Buttons
- Byzantine Empire
- Cabbage
- Cacophony
- Cacti
- Caipirinha
- Cajole
- Calamari
- Calligraphy
- Calliope
- Callow
- Calm
- Calumny
- Campaign
- Camry
- Candidate
- Candy Land
- Canilla
- Canines
- Cannoli
- Canola Oil
- Cantonese
- Canvas
- Capacitor
- Capicola
- Cappuccino
- Capricious
- Captain
- Captivating
- Cardamom
- Cardigans
- Caricature
- Carnation
- Carpenter
- Carrot
- Cashews
- Castle
- Catalyst
- Catfish
- Cathexis
- Cattle
- Caucus
- Caviar
- Cayenne
- Cedar
- Celebrate
- Celerity
- Celery
- Celesta
- Cellphone

- Celluloid
- Cenotaph
- Censorship
- Centaur
- Ceramics
- Cerberus
- Cetaceans
- Chagrin
- Chainsaw
- Chairperson
- Chalcedony
- Challenge
- Champagne
- Champion
- Chaotic
- Charades
- Charcoal
- Chard
- Checkdown
- Checkers
- Checking
- Cheeks
- Cheerios
- Cheetahs
- Chelonian
- Cherokee
- Cherry
- Chess
- Chevrolet
- Chhena
- Chicanery
- Chicken
- Chickpeas
- Chicory
- Chief
- Chimera
- Chinatown
- Chine Coat
- Chinese
- Chisel
- Chives
- Chocolate
- Chokers
- Choose
- Choreography
- Chorizo
- Chromatic
- Churlish
- Churros
- Cilantro

- Cimmerian
- Cinematic
- Cinnamon
- Cinquain
- Circuit
- Circuit Board
- Cirrus
- Citation
- City
- Cityscape
- Cladding
- Clams
- Clarify
- Clarinet
- Classicism
- Classroom
- Clean
- Clematis
- Climb
- Clinquant
- Clock
- Closed
- Closer
- Clotho
- Clouds
- Cloves
- Clownfish
- Cloying
- Clumsy
- Coach
- Coalesce
- Cocktails
- Coconut
- Coffee
- Coffee Cup
- Cogent
- Coiling
- Cold
- Collaborate
- Collage
- Color
- Color Print
- Color Spectrum
- Color Wheel
- Colorful
- Column
- Combine
- Comfortable
- Commander
- Commemorate

- Commission
- Communicate
- Compass
- Compasses
- Compete
- Complaint
- Complementary
- Complex
- Compose
- Composer
- Composition
- Computer
- Computers
- Concentric
- Conceptual
- Conch
- Conciliator
- Conductor
- Confident
- Conflate
- Confront
- Confucius
- Confuse
- Connect
- Connector
- Conquer
- Conqueror
- Conservator
- Construct
- Constructivism
- Constructor
- Consultant
- Continue
- Contour
- Contract
- Contrail
- Contrite
- Controller
- Conveyor
- Convivial
- Cookies
- Cooking
- Coordinate
- Coordinator
- Copious
- Coriander
- Corn Oil
- Cornet
- Cornflakes
- Corolla

Coruscate
Costume
Coterie
Cottage
Counselor
Counterfeit
Couscous
Coverts
Cowardly
Cowpeas
Coyotes
Crackers
Crackling
Cramped
Cranberry
Craniotomy
Crayfish
Crayon
Crayons
Crazing
Crease
Create
Creative
Creator
Credulity
Crepes
Cricket
Critique Cropping
Croissants
Cronus
Crosstrek
Crowbar
Cruel
Crush
Cry
Cubism
Cucumber
Cufflinks
Cuisine
Cultural Icon
Culture
Cumin
Cumulus
Cupcakes
Curator
Curious
Custodian
Customs
Cute

Cyborgs
Cycling
Cyclops
Cymbals
Cynosure
Dachshund
Daffodil
Daikon
Daiquiri
Damages
Dance
Dance Off
Dark
Dassault
Dawn
Dearth
Debate
Decapitate
Decide
Decimate
Decorative Arts
Decrease
Deep Sea
Defeat
Defendant
Defender
Defenseman
Delightful
Demagogue
Demeter
Demolish
Denouement
Deposition
Describe
Desiccate
Design
Designer
Despise
Destiny
Destroy
Desultory
Deteriorate
Deuce
Devastate
Develop
Developer
Devour
Diaphanous
Dichotomy
Dietitian

Difficult
Diffident
Digital Age
Dilatory
Dimensional
Dinosaurs
Diode
Dionysus
Dip Pen
Diplomat
Diptych
Director
Dirty
Disappear
Disarm
Disbelieve
Disconnect
Discordant
Discover
Discovery
Disembowel
Dishonest
Disintegrate
Dislike
Dismantle
Disorganize
Disparate
Dispatch
Disperse
Displeasing
Disquiet
Diving
Division
Documentary
Dodgeball
Dolls
Dolphins
Donuts
Doodlea
Doubles
Doubt
Doughnuts
Downtown
Drab
Draconian
Draftsman
Dragon
Dragons
Draw
Draw Play

Drawing
Dream
Dresses
Drive
Driver
Drones
Drop Shot
Dropout
Drum Set
Dry Foot
Dry Point
Duck Fat
Duckweed
Dugongs
Dulcimer
Dull
Dumb
Dungeons
Duplicity
Durian
Dusk
Dwarf
Eagles
Earphones
Earrings
Earthwork
Easels
Easy
Eat
Ebullient
Eccentric
Ecdysiast
Echeveria
Eclairs
E-Commerce
Economics
Edamame
Edentates
Edging
Edit
Education
Educator
Effulgent
Eggplant
Eggshells
Egregious
Egyptian
Einkorn
Elantra
Eldritch

Elector
Electronics
Elegant
Elegy
Elephants
Elevation
Elicit
Eloquent
Elucidate
Elusive
Embrace
Embroidery
Empanadas
Empathy
Empty Gaze
Empty Nest
Empty Soul
Enchanted
Enchanting
Encomium
End
End Zone
Endive
Endoscopy
Enforcer
Engage
Engineer
English
Engobe
Engraving
Enigmatic
Enlargement
Ephemeral
Epic
Epigram
Epimetheus
Epiphany
Epistolary
Equinox
Eradicate
Erasers
Erato
Eremite
Erinyes
Eros Love
Erupt
Escape
Escarole
Esoteric
Espalier

Espionage
Espresso
Etching
Ethereal
Ethics
Euchre
Euphemism
Euphonium
Euterpe
Evanescent
Evidence
Evocative
Evolution
Evolve
Examiner
Excel
Exciting
Exclude
Execute
Exhausting
Exigent
Exit Poll
Exorcist
Exordium
Expand
Expensive
Explain
Explore
Explorer
Express
Expression
Expressionism
Expunge
Exquisite Corpse
Exterminate
Extinguish
Extirpate
Eye Bolt
Fabricator
Facade
Face
Face Mask
Faceoff
Facetious
Facilitator
Faded
Fail
Fair Ball
Fake
Family

Fantasy
Farmer
Farming
Farro
Fast
Fat Bikes
Fates
Fatigue
Fatuous
Fauna
Fauvism
Feckless
Fecund
Felicitous
Felines
Felony
Feminism
Feminist Art
Fencing
Fender
Fenghuang
Fennel
Fenugreek
Fervid
Fiction
Field
Fighters
Figurative
Figure
Fijian
Filigree
Filipino
Filming
Filmjölk
Finish
Finisher
Fire Axe
Fire Hose
Fire Pump
Firing
Fish Oil
Fishing
Fix
Flatworms
Flax Milk
Flaxseeds
Flexible
Flora
Florid
Flounder

Flowers
Flummox
Flute
Fly
Fly Ball
Foment
Font
Food
Football
Footwork
Foppish
Force Out
Forecheck
Foreground
Forehand
Forester
Forget
Form
Formal
Forsythia
Forte
Forward
Foul Ball
Found Objects
Founder
Fractious
Fragrant
Frames
Freeboard
Freekeh
Freeze Tag
French
Frenesi
Fresh
Frontier
Frost Date
Fruit Bat
Fruits
Fudge
Fugacious
Fulminate
Fumble
Funky
Funny
Furies
Furtive
Futurism
Gainer
Galaxies
Garbanzo

Garden
Gardens
Garlic
Garrulous
Garters
Gel Pen
Gelato
Generous
Genial
Genie
Genre
Gentle
Geoduck
Geometric
Gerbera
German
Germane
Germany
Gesture
Ghazal
Ghost
Gimcrack
Ginger
Giraffes
Girdles
Give
Gizzards
Gladiator
Gladiolus
Glaucous
Glaze
Glorious
Gloves
Go Fish
Goalie
Goaltender
Godfather
Golden Sun
Goldfish
Gorgon
Gorillas
Gouache
Graduate
Graffiti
Grains
Granola
Graphic
Grasses
Great Dane
Greedy

Green Peas
Green Tea
Greenware
Gregarious
Griffin
Grits
Groundbreaker
Guacamole
Guardian
Guess Who
Guide
Guilty
Guitar
Hacksaw
Haddock
Hades
Haiku
Hair Clips
Hair Ties
Hair Bands
Halibut
Hammer
Handbags
Handle
Handsaw
Happy
Haptic
Harangue
Harbinger
Hard
Hardboard
Harlem Renaissance
Harm
Harmonica
Harmony
Harsh
Hat Trick
Hate
Head
Headbands
Health
Healthy
Heap Sort
Heart
Heavy
Hedgehogs
Hedonist
Hegemony
Heliotrope

Helmet
Helmets
Helpless
Hemp Milk
Hemp Seeds
Heracles
Herbalism
Hercules
Heresiarch
Herring
Hestia
Heterodox
Hex Bolt
Hey Jude
Hide
Hieroglyphics
Hijabs
Hiking
Hircine
Historic
Historical
History
Holding
Holiday
Home Run
Honda
Honest
Hoodies
Hooking
Hopscotch
Horizon Line
Hornwort
Horses
Host
Hot
Hot Potato
Hot Sauce
Huddle
Hue
Hull Speed
Human Body
Humanoids
Humans
Humble
Hummus
Humor
Hydra
Hydrangea
Hyperion
Hyraxes

Hysterical
Hyundai
Ice Age
Ice Cream
Ice Fog
Iced Tea
Icicles
Iconic
Iconoclast
Iconography
Idealism
Idle
Idol
Illustrate
Illustrious
Imaginative
Imagine
Immutable
Impala
Impasto
Implementer
Impoverished
Impress
Impressionism
Impreza
Improve
Improvisation
Incandescent
Inception
Inchoate
Incinerate
Incline
Include
Increase
Incumbent
Inductor
Industrial
Ineffable
Inexpensive
Inflict
Information
Inimical
Iniquity
Innovation
Innovator
Insects
Insecure
Insidious
Insipid
Inspector

Installation
Instigator
Institutional
Instructor
Insurance
Intaglio
Integrate
Intelligent
Interact
Interaction
Intercessor
Interior Design
International
Internet
Intertitle
Intestines
Intimacy
Intrepid
Intricate
Inveigh
Inventive
Inventor
Inveterate
Invigorating
Invincible
Involve
Irascible
Irksome
Ironman
Irrepressible
Isthmus
Italian
Jack Beans
Jackalope
Jackals
Jackets
Jackfruit
Japanese
Jasmine
Jazz Age
Jell-O
Jellyfish
Jetstream
Jettison
Jewelry
Jicama
Jubilant
Judge
Judgment
Juggling

Jump
Jump Rope
Jumpsuits
Juncture
Juniper
Juxtapose
Juxtaposition
Kalimba
Kamut
Kangaroos
Karaoke
Karate
Karl Marx
Karma
Kashi
Kayaking
Keeper
Kenning
Ketchup
Khoya
Kia Forte
Kia Soul
Kickoff
Kidney
Kielbasa
Kikuyu
Kiln Wash
Kimchi
Kimonos
Kind
Kinetic
Kinetograph
Kinetoscope
Kitsune
Kiwano
Knowledge
Koalas
Kohlrabi
Kombucha
Korean
Kraken
Labneh
Labyrinthine
Lachesis
Lacquer
Lacrosse
Lacuna
Ladder
Lag Bolt
Lagniappe

Lakota
Landscape
Language
Languid
Laptop
Lasagna
Lassitude
Latte
Laugh
Lavender
Lawsuit
Lawyer
Leader
Learjet
Learn
Lease
Leeches
Leeward
Legacy
Leggings
Legumes
Lemonade
Lemon-Lime
Lemurs
Lentils
Leopards
Let It Be
Lethargy
Lettuce
Level
Leviathan
Lexicon
Lexus
Librarian
Life Raft
Life Ring
Lifeless
Light
Light Bulb
Lighthouse
Like
Lima Beans
Lima Peru
Limerick
Liminal
Line Drawing
Line Drive
Lingerie
Lion King
Lissome

Listen	Mandarin	Mixed Media	Neckties	Onion
Literature	Mandolin	Mnemonic	Nectarine	Only You
Lithe	Mango	Mnemosyne	Nefarious	Opaque
Lithography	Manhattan	Model	Negative	Open
Lively	Mania Love	Modem	Neglect	Open Book
Liver	Manifesto	Moderator	Negotiator	Open Door
Lizards	Manticore	Modern	Negroni	Open Heart
Loafers	Manufacturer	Mojito	Nemesis	Open Road
Lobotomy	Maori	Mollify	Neoclassical	Open Sky
Lobsters	Marathon	Mollusks	Neoimpressionism	Opener
Loch Ness	Marbles	Mondegreen	Neophyte	Operation
Logomachy	Marco Polo	Monitor	Nessie	Oppose
Loquat	Margarine	Monkeys	New Objectivity	Opulent
Lose	Margarita	Monochrome	Newts	Oracle
Lost Soul	Marigold	Monopoly	Nigerian	Orange
Loud	Marimba	Montage	Night Sky	Orangutans
Love	Marina	Mood	Nihilism	Orchid
Love Games	Marjoram	Moonbow	Nissan	Ordinary
Love Lost	Markers	Mooring	No-Hitter	Oregano
Love Story	Marsupials	Moribund	Noisy	Organic
Luminous	Martians	Mosaics	Nojito	Organize
Luster	Martini	Mosses	Nordics	Organizer
Lychee	Masks	Motif	Nostalgia	Origami
Maasai	Material	Motivator	Notebook	Originator
Macan	Matrix	Mountains	Noxious	Ostentatious
Macarons	Mattock	Mousse	Numbers	Ostrich
Mackerel	Maudlin	Muesli	Numinous	Ostriches
Maelstrom	Mayan	Muffins	Nutritious	Otters
Magic Lantern	Mayday	Mulberry	Nymph	Outback
Magical	Meatballs	Multiple	Oat Milk	Overcome
Magnanimous	Mechanic	Mural	Oatmeal	Overglaze
Mahi-Mahi	Mediator	Muse	Obelisk	Overhead
Mahogany	Medicine	Mushrooms	Obfuscate	Overpower
Mai Tai	Medium	Music	Oblique	Overseer
Maim	Melancholy	Mussels	Obliterate	Overtake
Main Sail	Melodrama	Mustang	Observe	Overtime
Maintainer	Melpomene	Mustard	Observer	Overwhelm
Majolica	Memoir	Mustelids	Ocean Waves	Oysters
Maker	Mentor	My Way	Oceanus	Pacemaker
Malibu	Mermaid	Myopic	Octopus	Paint
Malinger	Merz	Mystery	Octopuses	Paintbrush
Malleable	Messy	Mystical	Odious	Painting
Mallet	Metaphysical	Nadir	Odysseus	Palette
Malodorous	Métis	Naive	Odyssey	Palette Knife
Mammals	Mild	Narrative	Offside	Palliate
Mammatus	Millet	Nascent	Old	Palm Oil
Mammogram	Minimalism	Navajo	Old Master	Paloma
Manager	Minotaur	Neat	Olive Oil	Palpable
Manatees	Mint Julep	Nebulous	Onerous	Pan Flute
Mandala	Miscreant	Necklaces	One-Timer	Panacea

Panamera
Pancakes
Pancetta
Paneer
Panel
Pangolins
Panning
Panorama
Panties
Pantoum
Pants
Papaya
Paper Curls
Paper-Mâché
Paprika
Paradigm
Paralegal
Paranoiac
Parenting
Parfait
Paris
Parole
Parrots
Parsley
Parsnip
Participate
Partridge
Passat
Pastels
Pastries
Pathfinder
Patron
Patterns
Pavlova
Pea Milk
Peacemaker
Peach
Peanuts
Pecan Pie
Peculiar
Pecuniary
Pedantic
Pegasus
Penchant
Pencil
Pendants
Penetrating
Penguins
Pensive
Penurious

Peony
Pepperoni
Perennial
Performance
Performer
Periscope
Perseus
Persian
Persimmon
Pervasive
Perversion
Petulant
Pheasant
Phenom
Philosopher
Phoenix
Pholidota
Photogram
Photograph
Photojournalism
Photomontage
Photos
Photostat
Pianist
Piano
Piccolo
Pickles
Pickoff
Pictograph
Pictorialism
Picture Frame
Picture Plane
Pigment
Pilatus
Pileus
Pilot
Pinching
Pineapple
Pioneer
Pique
Pixels
Pizza
Plaintiff
Plan
Plane
Planner
Plantain
Planter
Plants
Plastic

Plate
Platform
Platitude
Plato
Play
Play-Doh
Plethora
Pliable
Pliers
Plumber
Plunder
Plywood
Poetry
Poignant
Pointillism
Polaris
Polemic
Police
Polished
Polite
Politics
Pollock
Polyethylene
Ponchos
Poodle
Poor
Pop Art
Popcorn
Poppy
Popular
Pop-Up
Porcelain
Porpoises
Porsche
Portent
Porthole
Portrait
Portuguese
Pose
Poseidon
Positive
Postmodernism
Potato
Pottery
Power Play
Powerful
Precedent
Preceptor
Precipice
Prehistoric

Preschool
Prescient
Preserver
Pretzels
Primary Color
Primates
Prime
Primitive Art
Print
Printer
Pristine
Prius
Probation
Prodigal
Producer
Professor
Profile
Profundity
Progeny
Prolix
Prometheus
Promulgate
Prop
Propaganda
Proportion
Propriety
Prosciutto
Protean
Protector
Prototype
Pruning
Pry Bar
Psycho
Pudding
Puerile
Pugnacious
Pummel
Pumpkin
Pungent
Puppetry
Purses
Pursue
Puzzles
PVC Pipe
Quagmire
Quechua
Quell
Querulous
Question
Quiet

Quill Pen
Quilting
Quince
Quinoa
Quirky
Quixotic
Quotidian
Rabbit
Rabbits
Racquet
Radiant
Radicchio
Radish
Rafale
Rain
Rambutan
Rancor
Rapacious
Raspberry
Ratchet
Ravage
Ravioli
Raze
React
Read
Readymade
Realism
Realistic
Receive
Reckless
Recondite
Recorder
Recount
Rectrices
Red Line
Red Wine
Red Zone
Redhot
Redolent
Redwood
Referee
Referendum
Refractory
Regress
Regulator
Reject
Relax
Relegate
Relics
Religion

Remember	Rude	Sea Urchin	Show	Snapper
Remiges	Rulers	Seafood	Showers	Sneakers
Renaissance	Run	Sear	Shred	Snow Peas
Rendering	Rutabaga	Seascapes	Shrewd	Snowfall
Repartee	Ryegrass	Seaweed	Shrews	Snowy
Replica	Saab 340	Secondary	Shrikhand	Sobriquet
Represent	Sad	Secret	Shrimp	Soccer
Representative	Safeguard	Secretary	Shrubs	Sociology
Reprobate	Saffron	Secure	Shutout	Socks
Reptiles	Sagacious	Sedge	Shutter	Socrates
Repudiate	Sailing	Sedges	Sibilant	Soft
Repulsive	Salami	Seditious	Siblings	Soil Ph
Resilient	Salient	Sedulous	Sideline	Solitude
Resist	Salmon	Seeder	Silent	Solve
Resistor	Salty Dog	Seedling	Silver Print	Solvent
Resourceful	Samoan	Segway	Silverado	Somali
Respect	Sampler	Seitan	Simple	Somnolent
Resplendent	Sandals	Self-Help	Sincere	Sonata
Respond	Sander	Self-Love	Sinecure	Sonnet
Rest	Sangria	Self-Portrait	Sing	Soporific
Restive	Sanguine	Selkie	Singapore	Soprano
Retail	Santa Fe	Semblance	Singles	Sorbet
Reticent	Sardines	Sentra	Sioux	Sorento
Retreat	Sardonic	Serene	Sirenia	Sorghum
Revise	Sarees	Serenity	Sirens	Sound Effects
Revolve	Sartorial	Serious	Sirius	Sour
Rhizome	Sasquatch	Serpent	Sisyphean	Sower
Ribald	Satellite	Service	Site-Specific	Sowing
Rice Milk	Satire	Sestain	Skates	Soy Milk
Rich	Satyr	Sestina	Skeleton	Soy Sauce
Rigel	Sausage	Set-Dresser	Skiing	Soy Yogurt
Rigid	Saxophone	Setting	Skipping	Soybeans
Rings	Scale	Sgraffito	Skylane	Spacious
Roadster	Scallops	Shade	Skylight	Spanish
Roadsters	Scanner	Shamisen	Slapshot	Sparrows
Robes	Scarves	Shape	Slay	Special Effect
Robotics	Scene	Share	Sleep	Special K
Robotics	School	Sharks	Sleepwear	Specious
Robots	Science	Shatter	Sloths	Spectrum
Rococo	Sci-Fi	Shawls	Slovenly	Spelt
Rodents	Scintilla	Sherwanis	Slow	Spices
Roman Art	Scintillating	Shih Tzu	Small	Spicy
Romance	Scones	Shiny	Smart	Spinach
Rompers	Scorpions	Shirts	Smartwatch	Spinnaker
Rosemary	Scrabble	Shooting	Smash	Spirits
Rotate	Scrimmage	Shootout	Smile	Spleen
Rough	Scrutinizer	Short	Smite	Spokesperson
Roughing	Sculpt	Shortening	Smoothies	Sponsor
Router	Sculpting	Shorts	Snails	Sportage
Rudder	Sculpture	Shovel	Snakes	Sports

Sprinkler
Spurious
Squash
Squid
Squirrels
Stain
Stain Glass
Stale
Stalwart
Star Wars
Starboard
Starfish
Starfruit
Start
Starter
Statute
Steam Fog
Steel
Stencil
Stern
Stevia
Steward
Stick
Stimulator
Stingy
Stir-Fries
Stockings
Stoicism
Stonehenge
Stoneware
Stop
Stratus
Strawberry
Streams
Street Photography
Strikeout
Strobe
Strong
Stud Bolt
Study
Stultify
Style
Stylized
Stylus
Subaru
Subconscious
Subdue
Subjugate
Sublime

Submit
Subpoena
Subterfuge
Succeed
Succeeder
Summons
Sun Spots
Sunflower
Sunny Day
Super
Super Pac
Supervisor
Support
Supporter
Suprematism
Surfing
Surgeon
Surreal
Surrealism
Surreptitious
Surveyor
Sustainer
Sweaters
Sweet
Swim
Swimming
Swimwear
Swing Sets
Switch
Swordfish
Sybarite
Sycophant
Synchronize
Tabasco
Tablet
Taciturn
Taco Cups
Tacoma
Taekwondo
Tag-Up
Takedown
Talk
Tall
Tallow
Tame
Tangerine
Tanka
Tantalize
Tapirs
Tarragon

Tasteless
Tasty
Tautology
Tea Bags
Tea Ceremony
Teach
Teacher
Technology
Teenagers
Telegraph
Telephone
Tempeh
Tenacious
Tenebrous
Tengu
Tennis
Tenor
Tequila
Testimony
The Bridge
The Style
The Trance
Themis
Theremin
Theseus
Think
Thinning
Thongs
Thriller
Tie Clips
Tiebreak
Tigers
Tight End
Tights
Tiguan
Tilapia
Timepiece
Timid
Timorous
Timpani
Tiramisu
Titanic
Tomato
Tom-Toms
Tongan
Tongue
Toppings
Topple
Topspin
Tote Bags

Touchback
Touchdown
Tourism
Toy Piano
Toy Story
Toyota
Trail Mix
Trailblazer
Trainer
Transcendent
Transistor
Travel
Traverse
Trees
Trellis
Tremulous
Trenchant
Trendsetter
Trial
Triangle
Triathlon
Trimming
Tripe
Triple
Tripping
Triticale
Trombone
Trotters
Trout
Trowel
Truculent
Truffles
Trumpet
Trust
T-Shirts
Tuber
Tucson
Tumultuous
Tunics
Turgid
Turkey
Turkish
Turmeric
Turnip
Turpitude
Turtles
Tutor
Twister
Type
Typewriter

Ubiquitous
Ukulele
Ultrasound
Umbrage
Umbrellas
Umpire
Unabashed
Unassailable
Uncomfortable
Unctuous
Undercut
Understand
Unfathomable
Ungulates
Unhealthy
Unicorn
Uniforms
Unique
Unleash
Uno Moss
Unrelenting
Untoward
Unyielding
Upbraid
Upholder
Urad Dal
Urania
Urbane
Urostomy
Utilize
Utopia
Vaccines
Vacillate
Vagary
Valuable
Vampire
Vanilla
Vanish
Vanquish
Vapid
Vaunted
Venerable
Venison
Veracity
Verbose
Verdant
Verdict
Vertigo
Vexing
Vhf Radio

Vilify
Villanelle
Vinegar
Violin
Visceral
Visionary
Vitiate
Vitreous
Vivid
Volley
Voluble
Voracious
Voter
Vulnerable
Waffle
Waffles
Walk
Walk-Off

Wallabies
Wallets
Wanton
Warrant
Warships
Watch
Watcher
Watches
Water Polo
Watercolor
Waterfall
Watermelon
Waterscape
Waterweed
Weak
Wealthy
Weasels
Wedging

Welder
Wendigo
Werewolf
Whales
Wheat
Wheaties
Wheel
Whimsical
Whiskey
Whittling
Wield
Wild
Wild Rice
Willow
Win
Windows
Windward
Winners

Wisteria
Wistful
Withering
Witness
Wizened
Wolves
Wombats
Work
Workers
Workshops
Worthless
Wraith
Wreak havoc
Wreck
Wrench
Wrestling
Write
Writer

Writhe
Xeric
Xhosa
Xyloid
Xylophone
Yesterday
Yogurt
Yonder
Young
Young People
Zamboni
Zealot
Zen
Zen Garden
Zephyr
Zephyr-like
Zero-Waste
Zestfest
Zoo
Zoo Animals
Zucchini

Congratulations, by now you've learned how to have fun while creating unique and exciting prompt images!

LYNN & RICHARD VOIGT

Artists, Authors, Educators, Inventors & Publishers

Paint Dreams - Sell Ideas - Market Messages

Look For More RIVO Book Titles Available On Amazon

DOODLING FOR ADULTS
Much More Than Just Another Coloring Book

DOODLE DESIGNS - Vol. 1
DOODLE DESIGNS - Vol. 2

SECOND OF FIVE - Lynn's Memoir - Episode #1
My Early Years - From Birth To High School

TWO BECOME ONE - Lynn's Memoir - Episode #2
Dating, College, Teaching & Marriage

SECOND OF FIVE AGAIN - Lynn's Memoir - Episode #3
Raising 3 Children & A Husband - COMING SOON!

BABY NAMES - 2014 Edition
32,250 Baby Names with Origins & Meanings PLUS
Top 100 Names & 2,000 Most Popular Names

GARDEN CONVERSATIONS
901 Garden Poems, Quotations, & Classic Words Of Wisdom

WI GARDEN - LET'S GET DIRTY
Promoting Tips, Tools & Techniques That Inspire
Gardeners Around The World

SEARCHING FOR SOUL
Simple Exercises That Can Help Clarify
The Meaning Of Life

QUOTATIONS ABOUT SOUL
500 Inspirational & Motivational Quotations
About Soul

The GOLDEN VAULT OF QUOTATIONS
Words Of Wisdom From The Greatest Minds & Leaders

HEADLINE STARTERS
175,000 Words The Paint Dreams, Sell Ideas
& Market Messages

MORE THAN WORDS
5000+ Market Phrases That Sell

HYPNOTIC PHRASING
WARNING - This Book Teaches You How To Grab Eyeballs

ACTION HEADLINES That Drive Emotions Vol. 1
5,000 Unique Phrases For Marketing Ideas
ACTION HEADLINES That Drive Emotions Vol. 2
5,000 Unique Phrases For Marketing Ideas
ACTION HEADLINES That Drive Emotions Vol. 3
5,000 Unique Phrases For Marketing Ideas
ACTION HEADLINES That Drive Emotions Vol. 4
5,000 Unique Phrases For Marketing Ideas
ACTION HEADLINES That Drive Emotions Vol. 5
5,000 Unique Phrases For Marketing Ideas
ACTION HEADLINES That Drive Emotions Vol. 6
5,000 Unique Phrases For Marketing Ideas

POWER PHRASES (Complete Series Vol. 1-10)
5,000 Power Phases That Trigger Greater Profits

FUNNY HEADLINES Vol.1
FUNNY HEADLINES Vol.1
3,500 Outrageous Silly Brain Toots

MONEY WORDS
Powerful Phrases That Million Dollar Copywriters Use
To Make Piles Of Cash On Demand

CURIOUS WORDS
15,800 Words That Expand Minds & Change Lives

CLICHE BIBLE
8,400 Cliches For Sports Fanatics & Lovers
Of Popular Expressions

IDIOMS - IDIOMS - IDIOMS
6,450 Popular Expressions That Put Words In My Mouth

INSPIRING THOUGHTS
That Inspire Happiness, Success & A Clearer
Understanding Of Life

MARKETING EYEBALLS
100 Ideas Than Can Add Unlimited Subscribers

MY LIFE MATTERS
Recording A Meaningful & Fulfiling Life

MY GRATITUDE JOURNAL
Loving Relationships, Health, Financial Independence
& So Much More

THE BEAUTY OF GRATITUDE
Attracting More Joy & Happiness Into Your LIfe

The AMAZING GRATITUDE JOURNAL
For Girls Who Love Having Fun

The GRATITUDE JOURNAL
For Men On A Succes-Oriented Mission

GRATITUDE JOURNEY
Experience The Magic Of Keeping A Gratitude Journal

The MAGIC INSIDE A GRATITUDE JOURNAL
Experience The Endless Gifts Of Life

The LIGHTHOUSE BUCKET LIST
Recording Great Memeories For Your LIghthouse Visits

The GARDEN GRATITUDE JOURNAL
Recording Precous Moments In Your Garden

MY SECRET DIARY - Love, Hope & Dreams

MY DARKEST THOUGHTS
Confronting Fear, Anxiety & Worry To Live Happier

DAILY RANTS
Turning Outrage Into A Power Tool For Change

THE MAGIC WISH LIST
Every Miracle Begins With Passion & Action

MY DREAM JOURNAL
Recording Dream Visions Before They Disappear

MY SKETCHBOOK
Exploring Creative Thoughts & Ideas

The DOODLE DUMPSTER
A Creative Playground For Your Mind

LET'S GET DIRTY
Playing In The Garden Soil

MY LITTLE BLACK BOOK
Keeping Track Of Important Contacts Offline

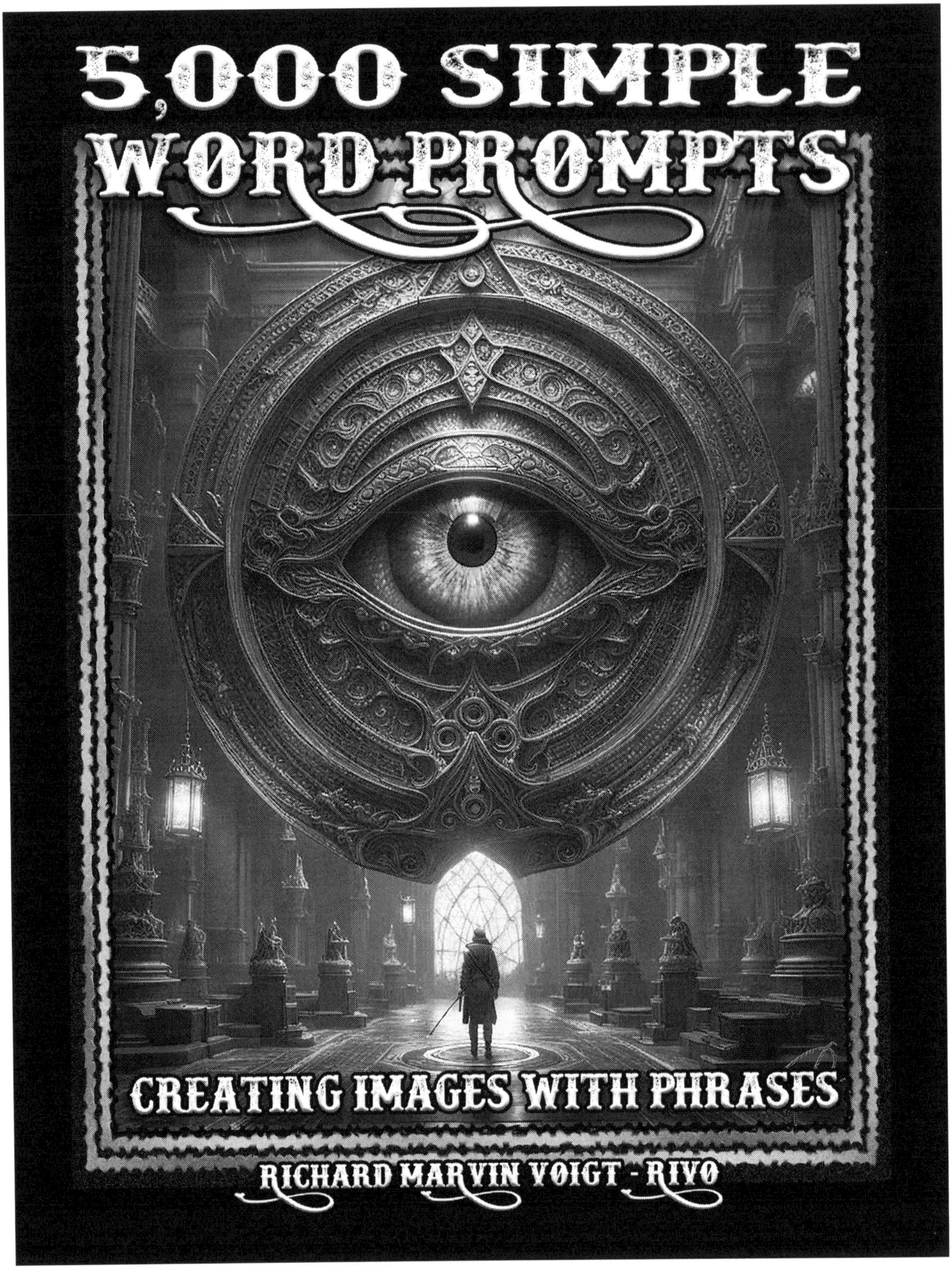
5,000 SIMPLE
WORD PROMPTS
CREATING IMAGES WITH PHRASES
RICHARD MARVIN VOIGT - RIVO

Thank you so very much for your interest and support in purchasing one of my latest publications. I always love hearing from my readers from around the world as to how this book may have helped you create more imaginative artwork.

While this educational publication is meant solely as a guide, you will constantly need to tweak your prompts as needed to accomplish the perfect image or idea you're after. These prompts are a great way to get started on your creative journey, whether you're an artist, author or simply seeking some great ideas. Enjoy your journey as you continue to refine, develop and releasing your unlimited imaginative powers.

Now it's up to you to begin or expand your AI Art adventures by refining and creating prompts that clearly illustrate the idea you have roaming inside your head. Finding appropriate words to build your AI prompts will become even more satisfying as you continue to create masterpieces, whether for personal enjoyment or business opportunities. Enjoy your journey!

I would deeply appreciate if you would take the time to leave an honest and candid review of this book at Amazon books. Simply, log into your Amazon account and enter the title:

"5000 SIMPLE WORD PROMPTS – Creating Images With Phrases"

I recommend creating a written review in a word document first, making spell-check easier. Then simply copy, paste and insert. Remember to click the submit review button to complete the review. Once the book title appears you will see a blue link that says, 'Customer Reviews,' Click it, and you'll be led to a new page and a button where you 'Create Your Own Review.'

Again, I sincerely want to thank you in advance for taking time to leave your review of this book on Amazon. It's because of you sharing your review that the word gets out to the rest of the world. "Keep The Love Growing."

Don't have an Amazon account? Feel free to email me **support@ART262.com.** I look forward to hearing from you and your prompt questions, as well as, your prompt successes.

Richard Marvin Voigt – RIVO

Check Out All Of My Word Prompt Publications:

"13,000 AI PROMPTS – Turning Words Into Visions" at Amazon Books
"5555 FUN & FUNNY PROMPTS Turning Words Into Images" at Amazon Books
"5000 SIMPLE WORD PROMPTS-Creating Images With Phrases" at Amazon Books

To Access Latest Publications, Artwork and Video Productions Visit:
www.ART262.com – www.DigitalArtPrintz.com - www.WisconsinGarden.com

Made in United States
Orlando, FL
04 November 2026

90201214R00057